ADVENTISM+

VOL.02:SYNTHESIS

MARCOS TORRES

Adventism+ Vol. 2.

Self-Published by Marcos D. Torres

ISBN: 978-1-7636905-2-3

For permissions or information contact:
pastormarcos@thestorychurchproject.com

Cover Designed by Andrew Caroll at, 42 Design

For more Adventist Missional Resources go to:

www.thestorychurchproject.com

Contents

Introduction

Welcome to Adventism+ Vol. 2: Synthesis. In the first volume, we reflected on the posthuman shift that our western, developed societies are currently undergoing. We set a simple foundation for understanding where we are and then embarked on an exploration of how fundamental beliefs 1 through 7 (doctrines of God, creation, and humanity) could be rearticulated to speak life and meaning into a world far removed from the horse-and-wagon days of our pioneers.

While much of my work focuses on postmodernism and Metamodernity as the prevailing cultural moods that missional believers must navigate in the secular west, in this series of books I aim to venture further—into the next 30 years of sociocultural and technological evolution.

The reason is simple. I'm tired of Adventists joking about how we are always 20 years behind the rest of the world.

It was funny the first time I heard it. It's not funny anymore.

In Volume 2, we are going to continue this exploration by focusing on fundamental beliefs 8 through 14 which include the Great Controversy theme, the gospel, the church, and the remnant.

The presuppositional groundwork and parameters for our exploration have already been laid in Volume 1, so I won't reiterate them here. If you have not yet read Volume 1, please do so in order to get the most out of Volume 2. This present volume is an extension rather than a repetition. We will build on the philosophical foundations already established.

However, there is one central concept that I want to emphasize as we continue our voyage. This concept, I believe, is the epicenter from which all of Adventism+ emerges: that while posthumanism describes a new world of technological convergence—a world in which artificial intelligence, genetic engineering, transhuman aspirations, multiplanetary migration, and life extension technologies redefine what it means to be human—*none of these capture what the movement is fundamentally about.*

Posthumanism isn't about a city on Mars. It's not about reversing aging. It's not about developing superintelligence or blending humanity with machines for the sake of evolutionary supremacy.

At its core, posthumanism is about vulnerability.

In other words, posthumanism is less a technological revolution and more an existential project. We dream of cities on Mars because life confined to one planet renders our species existentially fragile in the face of extinction-level events. We merge man with machine because the glacial pace of natural evolution threatens to leave us obsolete in the unforgiving mechanisms of survival. We reverse aging, pursue superintelligence, and explore the digitization of consciousness in our quest for digital immortality because, no matter how secular or post-religious we may become, we instinctively know the biblical truth that death is an enemy—an adversary to be conquered if humanity is to secure a future of enduring meaning and purpose.

Posthumanism, then, is driven by the same existential anxieties that underlie all self-redemptive religions. It represents an effort to save ourselves, to establish security against the chaos of existence, and to rage, as Dylan Thomas so eloquently put it, "against the dying of the light."

And here's why it's essential to restate this at the outset of Volume 2: Because like Volume 1, this present reading will not indulge in speculative or sensationalist explorations of how theology might be influenced by the next overhyped technological breakthrough. Such attempts are ultimately futile. Superintelligence could prove to be an empty promise. Elon Musk's Martian city may remain a distant fantasy. A nuclear war could catapult us back to the Stone Age, rendering all such discussions irrelevant.

The truth is, we have no certainty about how the posthuman era will manifest. Which aspects of it will thrive, and which will falter? Just a few years ago, the Metaverse was hailed as the future. Now it's a dormant concept. Yet with advancements in AI, it might resurface in ways we cannot yet foresee.

So, while writing a book on how theology might interact with specific emerging trends from Silicon Valley would be fascinating, it would also be shortsighted. These volumes would lose their relevance as soon as those trends fade or their promises collapse under the weight of unmet expectations.

What, then, is the wiser way to engage the posthuman world? It is to grapple with its anxieties. The technologies of posthumanism may come and go, but the existential promises they offer—security, transcendence, and mastery over vulnerability—remain enduring. These are promises that address humanity's deepest fears: fear of mortality, fear of cosmic indifference, and fear of the chasm of death. And it is these existential longings that we, as Adventist missionaries, must be prepared to engage in the posthuman epoch.

Thus, while this book is about the future, as in Volume 1, we will also revisit the past. We will converse with the existentialists who articulated the angst of the human condition in the shadows of modernity. Their questions remain deeply relevant as we reimagine how to present the beauty of Adventism to a world and an era that would short circuit Uriah Smith's and Joseph Bates' nervous systems. A mere glimpse of a mundane modern day, with tens of thousands of cars speeding through a complex array of coiling highways at over 100 kilometers an hour, skyscrapers reaching into the clouds with glowing lights, and fighter jets breaking the sound barrier as they unleash fire from heaven on their unlucky targets would be enough to overwhelm even our most revered pioneers.

Furthermore, in this volume I will continue to assert my conviction that a relational articulation of Adventism, framed by the Great Controversy narrative, holds unparalleled potential to address these cultural and technological shifts meaningfully. I believe we possess the most relevant theological framework for this dialogue—a framework unmatched by any other system. And yet, we are asleep. Trapped in time capsules of our own making, we address questions no one is asking, debate issues no one cares for, and squander the opportunity to unleash the power of our story.

I try to avoid hyperbole regarding Satan, but if I were him, I would work tirelessly to keep us ensnared in this irrelevant, tone-deaf, and self-destructive state. I would ensure that our voice is silenced, not by external opposition, but by our own inability to rise above the emotional fragmentation and internal conflicts we have become enamored with. This is the tragic reality of our movement today.

Yet, beyond this brokenness lies a narrative—a story that can soothe the existential dread fueling the posthuman quest. It offers relational depth, poetic resonance, collective and individual healing, moral clarity, and a vision of hope that far surpasses anything humanity's temples of stone, gold, or silicon could ever achieve.

That narrative is Jesus. That hope is Jesus.

And what we will discover in this second volume is that in him, we find a connected whole that brings the posthuman anxieties to a final resolution. Because it turns out, at the end of all our advancements and revolutions, there remains one center, one confluence, and one unifying principle in which the hope of the human species lies.

Put simply: Christ is our *synthesis*.

In him, the divine and the human become one again.

And consequently, all things are restored to the relational oneness of the original design.

This is gospel. This is redemption. This is our message.

Chapter 1:

RE-ENCHANTMENT

"Life can be wearisome and dreary because the world is indifferent to us."
– Kilroy J. Oldster

In 2003, the best-selling rap-rock band Linkin Park released a song that would become the anthem of many. It was titled "In the End" and began with rapper Mike Shinoda laying a pessimistic foundation as he rapped about the futility of trying, describing it as "wasting it all," only to have everything "[fall] apart" anyway. At that point in the song, lead singer Chester Bennington emerges with a poem steeped in darkness and cynicism. "I tried so hard, and got so far," he sings, "But in the end, it doesn't even matter. I had to fall, to lose it all. But in the end, it doesn't even matter."

The song is meant to be a poem depicting the sufferings of Chester's upbringing, but as is often the case with poetry, it never fully unveils its meaning. Instead, the listener is free to interpret and construct their own significance. Not only did my peers and I play the song on repeat, but we also drank deeply of its excessive nihilism. Somehow, Chester's cries for meaning–cries that tragically culminated in his suicide in 2017–comforted us and reminded us that, in some dark sense, there was beauty in that meaninglessness.

This perspective is an important one for Adventists to grasp. For many of us, life and destiny are seen through the lens of "the blessed hope." We adopt an enthusiastic approach to reality–one which Adventist-turned-atheist Ryan Bell has described as "hopefully naïve."[1] Therefore, despite this bright vision of the future, we must learn to contend with the dark mirage of contemporary culture and appreciate its complexity. When we do, we will discover not only the prose within its borders but also a means to present our redemptive narrative without the shallow naivety we often exude.

But let's fast forward a bit, because while this task may appear complex in a post-religious world of nihilistic absurdity, but the coming technological age will amplify the challenges faced by missional Adventism. Allow me a few moments to wrestle with the advent of augmented reality, how it relates to our quest for meaning, and the opportunities this presents for kingdom growth.

Augmented Reality as Quasi-Enchantment

In her 2025 Popular Mechanics article, "Transporting Your Consciousness to an 'Alternate Reality'...", journalist Stav Dimitropoulos wrote,

> [T]he line between reality and imagination has never been thinner. With social media, AI, and algorithm-fed content, we can live in a world where virtual existence isn't just an idea–it's a fully legit way of being.[2]

Dimitropoulos is articulating a profound and timeless human reality—that we are dual-dimensionally natured. Put simply, this means that we are made to inhabit two dimensions at once. The first dimension is the terrestrial, the immanent. We are built to be present to the earth, attentive to the moment, enraptured by our "shared nows." The other dimension is the celestial, the transcendent. We are likewise built to be present to the heavenly, aware of the eternal, and elevated by divinely ordained cosmic purpose. And all through history, humans have existed in this dual-dimensional state, particularly during what is known as the "pre-modern" era.

The pre-modern era describes the time before modernity. This chapter of the human story was dual-dimensional in that humans inhabited both a religio-spiritual and a secular/mundane world. The religio-spiritual was governed by mythos, legend, fantasy, or theology (depending on one's culture). The secular/mundane world was concerned with eating, planting, labor, and homemaking. But they were not separate worlds. They overlapped so much that philosopher Charles Taylor referred to this era as a time of "enchantment." The world, he says, was magical, charmed, and enchanted.

Then modernity arrived. And, as far as the West is concerned, with it came the end of enchantment. Modernity was only concerned with the tangible, the measurable, and the observable. It was naturalistic. As this worldview took control, society advanced technologically in ways not previously known, but it came at a cost. For the first time in history, human beings no longer experienced a dual-dimensional state. The celestial world was deleted.

The physical world stood alone. The universe was disenchanted. Humanity became mono-dimensional.

But here's the thing—human beings are not wired to be mono-dimensional. We are built for dual-dimensionality. The moment you reduce our world to a flat plane, you take away the transcendence that charms us. We become what Nietzsche referred to as "the last man"—those who look at the wonder of existence and merely "blink." It is in this state that the words of Chesters song make the most sense. In the end, nothing really matters. Why? Because once you exit this dimension, there is no other, no beyond. As "Dead Toad Scrolls" author Kilroy J. Oldster put it, "the world is indifferent to us."

Such a state of being is unlivable. The human psyche demands more. It clamors after more. But the Western world had already moved away from pre-modernism. The trauma left behind by the age of religion will not easily be forgotten. The world simply didn't want to go back. So, rather than return to the dual-dimensional dance of terrestrial and celestial fusion, we engineered a new dimension altogether. One that could take the place of the celestial. One that could fill the void and return a sense of the beyond to us. Enter the digital age.

Today, Western humanity is once more a dual-dimensional being. Only now, the dimensions are terrestrial and digital. The celestial is still on the edges, reserved for subcultural groups that dare to venture into ancient paths. For the most part, the secular West is a dual-dimensional world that inhabits two secular realities simultaneously. The digital world offers endless amusements, governed by a different set of rules, and allows one to construct entirely new identities. Meanwhile, the terrestrial world persists.

But remember, the goal of this dance is not to keep the two dimensions separate but to overlap them until they become one. Now, with the arrival of augmented reality, the lines between our synthetic digital dimension and our physical world become increasingly blurred. This, I believe, will usher in an era in which the nature of truth becomes an old, worn-out debate. The new debate will center on the nature of reality itself.

Innovators and tech CEOs like Mark Zuckerberg believe the advent of augmented reality and immersive computing will be beneficial. They argue it will allow us to no longer bounce back and forth between one dimension and another, as we currently do with external devices. Instead, augmented reality will layer the digital dimension over the physical, merging the two. Like pre-modern societies of old, we return to a reality defined by the natural and the other-than-natural. Only this time, the "other-than" is not enchanted. It is synthetic.

Time will tell what the full effects of such a move will be. But one thing is clear: social media, the centerpiece of the digital dimension, promised to connect us in unprecedented ways. It succeeded—but its success came at a cost. Hyper-connectivity has not led to deeper friendships or belonging. To the contrary, it has alienated us more than ever before. It's an ironic tragedy that we could be the most connected generation and simultaneously the loneliest. Augmented reality, for all its promises, is likely to push us further into extremes, overextending us beyond ourselves, deepening alienation, and amplifying our collective meaning crisis.

In fact, Dimitropoulos points out this very tension when she writes,

> AI isn't just fooling the eye anymore—it's creeping into cognition, subtly rewiring how reality is processed. And it doesn't stop there. AI-generated influencers like Lil Miquela and Shudu Gram blur the boundaries further, interacting, endorsing, influencing—as if they were real. What's illusion, what's not?

> Maybe it's easy to dismiss all this as nothing more than youthful imagination—kids caught in a digital daydream, destined to crumble under the obligations that come with adulthood anyway. But what if, by immersing themselves deeply enough in a fictional world, Gen Z brains start storing those experiences as real, longer-ter memories? What if—through repetition, rituals, and AI's surreal contact—Desired Reality, as shifters call it, starts implanting memories of its own while pushing Current Reality to the curb?[4]

Dimitropoulos's questions are profound and relevant. But I would counter by asking, what alternative is there? In a world that has abandoned the enchantment of the celestial dimension, an alternative must take its place. And in the face of this anxiety, this deep searching and longing, the missional believer must be prepared to offer a true alternative. An authentic re-enchantment that recognizes the failures of religion while inviting the culture back toward a true dual-dimensionality, one governed by depth and love rather than pixels and products.

Re-Enchantment Through the Great Controversy

It is at this juncture that I would like to offer a wild proposition. The above task of re-enchanting the world with a healing teaching that is both transcendent and immanent, that can be layered over our deepest agonies—not to solve, but to soothe—and through which we can re-inhabit a dual-dimensional existence that is spiritually rich, emotionally healthy, and culturally engaging, already belongs to us.

As an Adventist, I can think of no better lens through which to contend with the absurdity and beauty of life, as well as our culture's thirst for an enchanted, dual-dimensional resurgence, than the Great Controversy (which John Wesley aptly referred to as "scriptures aesthetic theme"). This theological motif is, by far, the most compelling and confronting approach to humanity's cosmic significance I have ever encountered. In all my conversations with secular minds, the Great Controversy stands out as one of the most exciting propositions to explore. When properly contextualized to the secular language of being, its resonance can be overwhelmingly profound.

Before diving into the meaning of the Great Controversy in light of life's absurdity, it is essential to point out the misuses of this motif. As is true of all doctrinal frameworks, constraining its narrative to religio-centric concerns is a sure way of neutering its capacity to engage meaningfully with today's secular world and tomorrow's posthuman era.

Regrettably, in many conversations I've had with Adventists, the Great Controversy is often stilted in just such a way. Consequently, it emerges as a theological lens we use to "explain away" tragedy, injustice, and suffering rather than as a lens through which we confront and contend with those realities. The number of times I've heard Adventists shrug off a social catastrophe with the classic, "We know why this is happening, brother—it's the Great Controversy," is enough to make me realize that we are, perhaps, missing the point altogether.

Similarly, some have weaponized the Great Controversy motif to embolden a narcissistic sense of self-importance, fueling lives obsessed with conspiracies. The justification? "There's a Great Controversy going on," as if this theological reality sanctifies an endless pursuit of speculative theories.

Finally, it has, at times, nurtured a cynical faith rivalling even postmodern dystopianism. I have often wondered if conservative Adventism's fixation on dreary apocalypticism has been somewhat shaped by the crumbs left behind via postmodernism's sardonic orientation.

Moreover, the Great Controversy is not a divine public relations campaign in which God tells humanity, "I know life can be hideously dark, but trust me—I didn't do it! The devil did." No, it is not a cookie-cutter formula meant to assuage every existential angst, nor is it an explanation to offer a grieving mother whose baby girl was born lifeless.

In this sense, the Great Controversy cannot answer every question or make sense of every incoherence of existence.

However, it can help us navigate pain toward what philosopher Martin Heidegger referred to as "the freedom to become myself."[3] It is more like a companion that unveils the goodness of God while wrestling with the tenebrosity of existence. Through it, we can craft music from the wildly complex variables of the war between good and evil. Through it, we can layer a new dimension of color over the monochromatic emptiness of our desperate world.

Properly approached, therefore, the Great Controversy holds tremendous potential for speaking meaningfully to our fragmented culture. It addresses questions of social injustice, the pursuit of equitable societies, and the dream of a world where humanity can unite at one table without exclusion. But it is more than this. The Great Controversy also offers us a means through which we can re-enchant our world and return society to a dual-dimensional existence that anchors us in divine-human interconnectedness, resisting the allure of the digitization of transcendent worldviews.

Thus, in my discussions with secular seekers, I approach the Great Controversy in three layers: the origin of the cosmic tear, followed by the ensuing cosmic vacuum, and ending with the restoration of cosmic harmony. In all of this, my aim is to offer both a present and future dreaming that fills the void left by modernity as well as soothes the fears left by religiosity. This chapter will cover the first of these layers; the subsequent chapters will explore the others.

The Origin of the Cosmic Tear

Where does evil come from? This is a question the Great Controversy seeks to contend with rather than resolve. For the question of evil is not one that allows for philosophical resolution. Here, I agree with Adventist pioneer Ellen G. White, who wrote, "If a cause be shown for its existence, it would cease to be sin."[5] Therefore, we must not claim more for the Great Controversy than it offers. It is not an "answer" in the conventional sense but rather a narrative pathway through which we can confront life with metaphysical confidence despite lingering mysteries.

As the Great Controversy unfolds, we encounter the question: Who is God? In Volume 1, we explored God's ontology through the apostle John's declaration, "God is love" (1 John 4:7). We observed that creation emerges from the overflow of divine love and is designed to reflect it. Creation was woven with threads of love, intended to afford humanity an eternal existence of limitless development—always rising, learning, and growing.

Yet, life as we know it does not reflect this original intent. A collapse occurred. The very fabric of reality was torn. We are now constrained by limitations that only our dreams can transcend. Screenwriter Stephen Karam described these as the "existential horrors of life" that "drive our imaginations and theatre."[6]

In the secular world, this reality is navigated through amusement, duty, and transcendence. These three approaches fuel modern society. They are its engine, driven by humanity's angst. The wandering human heart clings to amusement for escape, responsibilities to manufacture meaning, and transcendent ideologies to placate its insatiable desire for the beyond. Together, they sustain corporations supplying endless movies, careers, and self-help gurus to meet this demand.

But man remains empty. Given the right circumstances, these navigation systems can collapse in an instant, leaving us naked before the devouring abyss of existence, which seems intent on silencing our voice and returning us to nothingness. Kilroy J. Oldster captured this reality as "wearisome," "dreary," and "indifferent."

However, the Great Controversy offers an alternative perspective. Building on God's ontology of love and creation's purpose, it seeks to layer meaning over our suffering. In doing so, another being enters the narrative: a conscious power at war with God. Sometimes depicted as a dragon, serpent, angel, or accuser, this "ha satan" is identified as the originator of the cosmic tear we exist within.

Yet, such a proposition invites intuitive questions: If God is good and the universe is good, how did Lucifer conceive of bad? What was his reference point? And what is the purpose of freedom if Satan could only choose God? Without opposing options, how could Lucifer choose?

These questions are vital to understanding the cosmic tear. Lucifer's choice was not between a good God and an evil god—there was only God. Reality was entirely good. Lucifer's choice, therefore, was between God and not-God, between allowing God's presence to occupy its rightful space or removing God from that space. He chose not-God, pursuing an imagined "higher good" divorced from the Creator. What Lucifer may not have understood was that, as a derivative being, his existence depended on God's presence. By choosing not-God, he rent the nature of reality like a cloth, attempting then to stitch it back together with himself.

This absence of God's love became the animating force of Lucifer's being: his inner tear, which we often simplify under the label "self-centeredness." It disrupted heaven's harmony, leading to rebellion, war, and separation. And by joining Lucifer's rebellion, humanity placed itself under the same governing power of love's absence—the cosmic tear, the way of self. In doing so, the design of reality was likewise torn. Our world and its ecosystem destabilized. And from this tear, we find ourselves siphoned into a vacuum of corruption, empire, and injustice. The result is a new world governed by a new law, which engineers parasitic structures that benefit some at the expense of others. And there, we have the perfect recipe for more than mere suffering. Our world is now a conveyor belt, a factory, a machine that systematizes suffering at large.

Understanding this sets the stage for exploring the cosmic vacuum, which then leads us toward the promise of restoration that makes the Great Controversy such a potent worldview, capable of re-enchanting our world and delivering us from the spiritual anorexia of the age. We will turn to these themes in the next chapter.

_____

Notes

1. Ryan Bell, "Former pastor Ryan Bell on why he abandoned his Christian faith: I gave it my best shot," The Guardian, December 27, 2014. Available at: https://www.theguardian.com/world/2014/dec/27/former-pastor-ryan-bell-abandoned-christian-faith.

2. Stav Dimitropoulos, "Transporting Your Consciousness to an 'Alternate Reality' Online Could Cause Memory Problems, Scientists Say," Popular Mechanics.

3. Martin Heidegger, Being and Time, translated by John Macquarrie and Edward Robinson, Harper & Row, 1962.

4. Stav Dimitropoulos, "Transporting Your Consciousness to an 'Alternate Reality' Online Could Cause Memory Problems, Scientists Say," Popular Mechanics.

5. Ellen G. White, The Great Controversy, Pacific Press Publishing Association, 1888, p. 492.

6. Michael Paulson, "A Playwright Hits the Big Time: Stephen Karam on His White-Hot Career," The New York Times, November 22, 2015. Available at: https://www.nytimes.com/2015/11/22/theater/a-playwright-hits-the-big-time-stephen-karam-on-his-white-hot-career.html.

Vol. 2

Chapter 2:

VACUUM

"Do not go gentle into that good night. Rage, rage against the dying of the light."
- Dylan Thomas

The contemporary way of life is no longer sustainable. If something doesn't happen—and fast—humanity will go extinct. Thankfully, a solution has emerged due to a remarkable technological and scientific discovery. The solution is collectively known as "downsizing" and involves undergoing a medical procedure that reduces a person's size to 5 inches tall. The downsized person is then transferred to a community built for miniature humans—communities that are so small their ecological footprint is minuscule. If enough humans undergo the procedure, the impact of issues like overpopulation, dwindling resources, and global warming will practically disappear. It's a genius idea that can—quite literally—save the human species.

Now of course, the idea is not real. The technological advancement that makes this ludicrous proposal possible only exists in the script for the 2017 sci-fi film *Downsizing*, starring Matt Damon. According to the plotline, "downsizing" is the most humane solution for the future of humanity. Unfortunately, as the movie progresses, we discover that the solution doesn't actually work; not because it's a flawed proposition but because, in the end, only 3% of the population agrees to downsize. As a result, polar ice melting in the Arctic releases huge quantities of methane, making the air unbreathable and marking the end of human civilization. To give humanity a fighting chance, a small company of downsized humans descends into a geothermal bunker designed to house them and their posterity for the next 8,000 years—the amount of time it will take for the earth's surface environment to restabilize.

Apart from the fact that the film received a much-deserved 48% review on Rotten Tomatoes (it was really bad), one scene in particular resonated with me. As the band of survivors prepares to descend into the vault, the "inventor" of downsizing says:

> "Yes, we are sad to leave. And terribly sad for the reasons why. But man is too beautiful, too improbable a lifeform, to be allowed to disappear forever from the cosmos."

Romantic as the scientist's declaration may be, the beautiful man he speaks of is simultaneously the perpetrator of his own destruction. Only 3% of the earth's population cared enough—or bothered to believe—that something needed to be done for future generations. The rest did not seem bothered, and now, thanks to their indifference, the human race is marked for extinction. In light of this reality, another of the film's characters justifies his refusal to enter the bunker by saying:

> "You think they won't behave like people always behave? They're all going to go insane down there and kill each other. They'll go extinct long before we

do."

So, which is it? Is man a beautiful lifeform that must be preserved, or an insanely self-centered entity whose extinction is merited? The film never really answers the question. The best one can walk away with is that some people are worth saving and others are probably not. But then, how do we decide who is and who isn't? And if we saved all the right people, who is to say their offspring won't grow to repeat the errors of the past?

This possibility is hinted at when—while discussing the bunker—the main character likens it to Noah's Ark, which we all know was a temporary solution at best. It did not redeem humanity but simply reset its self-destructive path back to step one. And since then, we have been steadily repeating all the steps until, on June 16, 1945, the first atomic bomb was detonated. Since then, this weapon of mass destruction has evolved into a weapon of mass extinction and stockpiled in what are commonly known as "Nuclear Weapon States." The reality of nuclear war and complete human destruction now looms in our political subconsciousness—a reality kept at bay by diplomatic strategies that are as fragile as they are tenuous.

In the end, it seems the human race has one issue it cannot redeem itself from. It's what the late evangelist Billy Graham referred to when he said, "[The world is not] dangerous so much because we have atomic bombs. It's dangerous because of the human heart in back of the bombs, filled with envy and strife and greed and lust and all the other things that can pull the trigger."[1]

That is, man's greatest ill is not its weapons so much as its desire to create such weapons. There is a governing power in the human heart that brings with it a silent and underlying capacity that ironically makes our species the perpetrator of the very catastrophes we judge God for.

This governing power is the way of self. And this way became our way when the fabric of our reality was torn through rebellion. That cosmic tear damaged our world and our hearts so that now, rather than operating to the rhythms of love, we are driven by the impulse of self.

In the previous chapter, I explored how approaching the Great Controversy from the layer of this "cosmic tear" is imperative in connecting this theme with the secular mind of today and tomorrow. Rather than looking at it as a means through which we explain suffering away, we look at it as the means through which we layer redemptive meaning over the very things that make life tragic and unbearable. That is, Lucifer's rebellion tore reality. The original design of love is now replaced by a system of governance that functions only through the impulse of self. And this impulse is at the epicenter of fallen empire. It drives success, fuels triumph, and secures legacies. No human dynasty, corporation, or structure can ever advance if not driven by the impulse of self. This is the cornerstone of the satan's government and the key which separates his rebellious regime from the kingdom of God.

Once we understand this existential tear and its reauthoring of reality from love to self, we must then add another layer: the cosmic vacuum. We will explore this layer below and conclude with the final layer—the restoration of cosmic harmony. These three perspectives, when combined, reframe the Great Controversy from a doctrine that is strictly religio-centric to a doctrine that speaks hope. But hope in what way? Jordan Peterson captures the nature of being perfectly when he said:

> "Life is a very difficult business. It's fatal and it's full of suffering. And in order to make your way through all of that, you have to develop a relationship with something that's profound. And what could be more profound than the truth? What would you rather have on your side?"

In this chapter, I contend that an existential look at the Great Controversy gives us the very "profound relationship" and "truth" that Peterson speaks of. It offers our disenchanted culture a way to re-enchant without having to return to the old, worn-out paths of moralistic religion. It allows us to, once again, inhabit a dual-dimensional existence that is both terrestrial and celestial, layering the former over the latter, adding wonder, meaning, and purpose to an existence laden with trial and tragedy. The Great Controversy—what John Wesley referred to as "scripture's aesthetic theme"—is cosmological equipment enabling us to—as Rollo May put it—"take meaninglessness and force it to mean."

The Cosmic Vacuum

The cosmic tear speaks of how reality was broken through rebellion. The original design of love and other-centeredness has been torn in half. But once that tear takes place, it needs to be filled. That gap that is left is essentially a vacuum. Vacuums demand satiation. And ever since the dawn of the tear, humankind has attempted to satisfy the demands of that vacuum. The first hint we find is in Genesis 3:7:

> "Then the eyes of both of them were opened, and they realized they were naked; so they sewed fig leaves together and made coverings for themselves."

The fig leaves become an emblem of all human attempts at satiating that vacuum. But think about it: Adam and Eve didn't snap their fingers and cloaks of fig leaves appeared. This was a task that would have taken them time to figure out. They had never had need of it before. There was no instruction manual. No template for them to follow. No YouTube tutorial. In order to design this covering, they would have had to innovate.

With a basic sketch in mind, the next step would be gathering enough leaves, and then finally, sewing them together. I doubt they had a packet of nylon string sitting in their pantry, which means they likely would have had to figure out how to make string using natural resources.

Finally, how to weave everything together with enough precision that the leaves wouldn't tear the moment the string tightened. All this is to say, Adam and Eve were engaged in the biggest, most stressful project of their lives. The vacuum roared at them with its emptiness. It demanded appeasement. And rather than turn to God, they did what they had now been re-programmed to do—they looked to themselves. They became the source of their own redemption.

But the thing with this vacuum is, it can't be satisfied, it can't be filled. It demands and demands—a bottomless pit with no end. You can never appease its wrath. But we try and we try. And the more we try, the deeper we sink into it until our entire existence is itself a vacuum in which the only thing that matters is the satisfaction of the self. It's a strange and fascinating thing that, in some non-verbal sense, we become one with the very vacuum we one day aimed to fill.

And here is why this matters, socially speaking. Because once that vacuum is in full effect, what you end up with is a man and a woman who can see no further than the self. The self becomes all. The self demands all. And when that man and that woman give birth to children, who give birth to children, who give birth to tribe, nation, and civilization where millions now traverse the plane of reality with the same tear and vacuum devouring them from within, what do you end up with?

Scripture's answer is simple: *empire*.

But we are getting ahead of ourselves. Before we get to empire, let's linger at the vacuum a little longer.

When we introduce the vacuum, we are entering, at last, the realm of human fallenness. Recall from our nature of man chapters that this view has to be carefully approached, avoiding the melodramatic and cynical view of man often associated with Calvinism and high-control fundamentalism, and instead affirming and celebrating the beauty of man.

Nevertheless, no exploration of biblical narrative can ever be complete without confronting the uncomfortable idea of sin. However, because of its history (the concept of sin has been used to abuse, coerce, manipulate, and control others), I hesitate to use this term until I have clearly defined what it means. Even then, I tend not to use it too much in order to maximize the person's ability to see with clarity the issues Scripture is addressing.

Because of this, I focus more on the root of sin rather than the particular three-letter word itself. And that root is the spiritual and existential vacuum that we, terrestrial beings, are born into. This vacuum may be mitigated and managed through education, self-development, and value structures that emphasize altruism, inclusivism, and charity—but in the end, the vacuum is always there and can never be fully eradicated. As a result, despite the incredible advancements in education, psychology, and ethics, horrid activities like slavery,[2] racism,[3] and other social ills are on the rise—almost like antibiotic-resistant infections.

It's this never-ending cycle of systemic injustice that led best-selling author Bernard Marr to ask, "Will AI Solve The World's Inequality Problem - Or Make It Worse?"[4]

Marr writes:

> Some believe AI can provide solutions to this by increasing efficiency and lowering costs, ultimately improving access to basic services and opportunities that can help people improve their lives. On the other hand, others believe that AI will exacerbate the problems faced by many of the world's poorest and

least advantaged, further funnelling access to wealth and resources to the few.

This tension over AI and social restoration/degradation is not new. It is a persistent problem going back as far as history allows us. Human civilization, for all its innovation, is stained by this perpetuation of the pattern of self and can be seen in small, seemingly imperceptible selfish actions we commit every day which, when multiplied exponentially, give birth to entire cultures, communities, and countries that are driven economically and socially by an impulse that includes some and excludes others, advances some and oppresses others, privileges some and victimizes others.

Consequently, even nations which today are regarded as champions of human rights are built on the subjugation and suffering of others: The land of the free and opportunity–the United States–with its displacement of Native Americans and participation in the global slave trade, which, for a time, was key to its economic success.[5] The lucky country–Australia–with its displacement of the indigenous peoples and stolen generations in which European colonialists, in league with the church, aimed to "breed the black" out of the natives.[6]

Europe–famous for its civilized and cultured class– simultaneously colonized islands and countries, oppressing the indigenous populations, robbing them of their sovereignty, and exploiting their resources.[7] Then there are corporations that profit from wars,[8] chocolate companies that profit from child labour,[9] fast fashion that exploits third-world workers in order to provide westerners with cheap, trendy clothes,[10] and jewelry companies that have long profited from conflict diamonds.[11]

I could go on and on, but again, these are macro-scenarios. One need not look that high to get a glimpse of the perpetuation of the impulse of self. One can simply look across the street. In the enlightened west, domestic abuse is on the rise,[12] as well as bullying and violence in school.[13] And then there is the most difficult place to look: the self. Look honestly enough and you will find that you, as a human being, have perpetuated suffering on this earth at some point in your life. We cannot help but hurt others or even ourselves. We lie, cheat, and manipulate; and even the kindest, most outward-focused ones among us live with the regret of botched opportunities, neglected chances, and wasted moments that have extended suffering around us. None of us are immune.

Is it true that many people today recoil at the mention of things like "sin"? Yes, but no. What people recoil against is judgmentalism and ethical coercion—things the church has done unchecked for far too long. But when speaking of the human capacity to amplify suffering—this the culture can resonate with. They see it everywhere and many oppose it through social justice movements that aim to construct a more equitable future for the marginalized. So, it's not sin's reality people need to be convinced of. Rather, what I have found the secular mind to be sometimes in need of is the realization that the problems of humanity are not simply "out there" but are fundamentally within.

Thus, a second layer is added to the Great Controversy. One which builds on the rebellion of Satan by, in some ways, moving beyond it far enough to say, "The devil didn't make us do it. We did it to ourselves." And from this layer, we can better grasp injustice and suffering as patterns of being in the world—patterns that emerge through complex interrelated events and culminate in trauma but which nevertheless originate within the very heart of man.

The Reversal of the Way of Self

However, one more layer remains which ties the entire narrative of the Great Controversy together and provides it with the relevance needed to connect with the secular mind: the grand reversal. What I mean by this is that God is on the move to reverse the way of self and he is actively doing it all around us. However, he is not seeking to establish a church full of rituals, a nation driven by policies, or a system organized by structures that agree with his ethical priorities. This is all meaningless in light of the fact that mankind's problem is not religious, national, or systemic. Mankind's real problem is impulsive—we are driven by an impulse that we perpetuate in repeated patterns until it gives birth to an assumed way of being in the world. This assumed way is the way of self, and none of us can avoid it.

For example, let's imagine a social worker actively involved in helping others and a warlord exploiting the vulnerable to advance himself. The social worker volunteers at the local soup kitchen and is, in all sincerity, a wonderful person. However, he is unknowingly trapped in the same "way" of injustice the warlord finds himself in. Thus, the social worker serves the poor and then uses his mobile phone to take a picture of all the smiling faces without realizing that his mobile phone exists as the result of economic exploitation that allowed the phone company to purchase the minerals from a mine in Congo.[14] And who sold them the minerals? Why the warlord who rapes and murders innocent people to maintain control over the region and line his pockets with western money. And that same social worker may even hand out clothes at the soup kitchen so that the poor can dress themselves and be warm–clothes manufactured in a factory in Bangladesh which collapsed and killed over 300 people because the company that hired them cut corners to keep costs as low as possible.[15]

And what can the social worker do about this? Is he to blame for the suffering? Should he refuse to buy a mobile phone or cheap clothes? And if he did–how would this help?

In truth, there is little to nothing the well-intentioned social worker can do. He is trapped in a system–a "way" of being–a way crafted and nurtured by a world driven at every angle by the impulse and pattern of self, a way so entrenched in the ebb and flow of human society that there is virtually no escape. As Martin Luther King, Jr. once said:

> "Injustice anywhere is a threat to justice everywhere. We are caught in an inescapable network of mutuality, tied in a single garment of destiny. Whatever affects one directly, affects all indirectly."[16]

Thus, the solution to this problem cannot be temporal. Man, as the perpetrator of the problem itself, cannot pretend to emerge as its solution. The solution must come from outside—from God. But if God is to resolve this problem, it will not be with religion. He will not fix it with ethics. He will not fix it with legislation. He must, instead, create an altogether different way. A way founded by perfect love and in direct opposition to Lucifer's government of self-centeredness.

This way must be patterned after perfect love, in opposition to man's perpetual patterns of self-centeredness. A way so pure, so entrenched in divine harmony that it does not, and indeed, cannot mingle with the way of self. This new way is thus a rebellion. It is counter-cultural. It refuses to conform to the unjust patterns of this world or to succumb to them.

In other words, God must fill the vacuum and mend the tear—first within our individual hearts, and then in the cosmos. This filling and mending is an act of resistance—a refusal to be absorbed. It is to roar back at a corrupted design that wants to swallow our very souls and stand, in the midst of its siphoning gusts, unperturbed, unmoved, and unafraid. It is to exist within the domain of this vacuum as an anomaly, anchored in divine love—a threat to the system's stability.

All of this culminates in the fullest realization of Dylan Thomas' famous poem: "Do not go gentle into that good night. Rage, rage against the dying of the light."[17]

This new way that rages against the darkness of human empire is the way of Jesus, through which our species experiences the restoration of cosmic harmony. It is what author Donald Kraybill referred to as "the upside-down kingdom." A new path founded in Jesus, patterned in Jesus, and etched in Jesus.

This way is not of this world; it is opposed to the systems of this world and is so other to this world that friendship with this world is enmity with the new way.

The people of the kingdom are thus invited to have the mind of Jesus, to not be conformed to the patterns of this world, but to be renewed by having their minds aligned to the way of other-centered love. This way is the way of Jesus, the way of light, the way of self-sacrifice, self-abandonment, and other-centered rhythm. It is a kingdom driven by the ethic of love, not the impulse of self.

And this kingdom of love is at war with the empire of self. Harmony is in conflict with the vacuum. The two will never mix. You cannot legislate the one into the other, for the kingdom of God is a kingdom of the heart. It is not a religious ideology, a political philosophy, or a governmental system. It is a way of being.

This way of being—this kingdom of love—the Bible declares will annihilate the impulse of self and, in the end, will reharmonize the cosmos, inverting the vacuum until the rhythm of giving replaces the pattern of taking. And this reversal has already begun.

This approach to the Great Controversy has significantly more meaning to a secular culture navigating the absurdity of life and being. It touches on the humanitarian heart of the age, on the cry for social justice and equity. However, it also challenges it.

The kingdom of God does not fit any earthly political campaign. It refutes the left and the right, the conservative and the liberal, the globalist and the nationalist. It exposes the entirety of human empire as a kingdom built on the impulse of self, maintained through the patterns that perpetuate self, and solidified as a way of self.

And then it promises one thing: a new kingdom is coming—not like all the others—built on the impulse of love, patterned after perfect love, and is itself, the way of love. This new kingdom will depose all the institutions and systems of this world and restore the universe to oneness with a God whose ontology is love.

This is the restoration of cosmic harmony—the culmination of the Great Controversy cosmology. Cosmic equipment for our meaning crisis. A celestial vision capable of re-enchanting our world by layering meaning and purpose over the very real inequities and injustices that we contend with.

Will such a vision be embraced by all? Never.

But can it offer the sincere, post-religious thinker something gallant on which to anchor her identity? Something richer than the quasi-enchantment offered by the hyper-commodified digital dimension we have built?

Undoubtedly.

———

Notes

1. Billy Graham, "The Cross – Billy Graham's Message to America," *YouTube Video*, https://www.youtube.com/watch?v=bba2Dqaw6SI.

2. Kate Hodal, "One in 200 People Is a Slave. Why?" *The Guardian*, https://www.theguardian.com/news/2019/feb/25/modern-slavery-trafficking-persons-one-in-200.

3. Rob Picheta, "Children 'Whitening Skin to Avoid Racism' as Hate Crimes Against Minors Rise," *CNN*, https://edition.cnn.com/2019/05/30/uk/britain-children-racism-hate-crime-gbr-intl/index.html.

4. Bernard Marr, "Can AI Solve the World's Inequality Problem or Make It Worse?" *LinkedIn Pulse*, https://www.linkedin.com/pulse/ai-solve-worlds-inequality-problem-make-worse-bernard-marr-rbuie/.

5. Greg Timmons, "How Slavery Became the Economic Engine of the South," *History*, https://www.history.com/news/slavery-profitable-southern-economy.

6. "Caught up in a Scientific Racism Designed to Breed Out the Black," *The Sydney Morning Herald*, https://www.smh.com.au/national/caught-up-in-a-scientific-racism-designed-to-breed-out-the-black-20080214-gds108.html.

7. Harry Magdoff, Richard A. Webster, and Charles E. Nowell, "Western Colonialism," *Britannica*, https://www.britannica.com/topic/Western-colonialism.

8. Samuel Stebbins and Evan Comen, "Military Spending: 20 Companies Profiting the Most from War," *USA Today*, https://www.usatoday.com/story/money/2019/02/21/milita ry-spending-defense-contractors-profiting-from-war-weapons-sales/39092315.

9. Peter Whoriskey and Rachel Siegel, "Cocoa's Child Laborers," *The Washington Post*, https://www.washingtonpost.com/graphics/2019/business /hershey-nestle-mars-chocolate-child-labor-west-africa.

10. "The True Cost," *Documentary*, https://truecostmovie.com.

11. Natalia Wojcik, "Conflict Diamonds May Not Be on the Radar, but They're Still a Worry for Some," *CNBC*, https://www.cnbc.com/2016/11/04/conflict-diamonds-may-not-be-on-the-radar-but-theyre-still-a-worry-for-some.html.

12. Sarah Marsh, "Domestic Abuse Offences in London Rise 63% in Seven Years," *The Guardian*, https://www.theguardian.com/society/2019/feb/27/domes tic-violence-london-rise.

13. Jennifer McClellan, "One Third of Middle- and High-Schoolers Were Bullied Last Year, Study Shows," *USA Today*,

https://www.usatoday.com/story/life/allthemoms/2018/09/24/one-out-three-students-were-bullied-us-school-last-year/1374631002.

14. Erin Banco, "Is Your Cell Phone Fueling Civil War in Congo?" *The Atlantic*, https://www.theatlantic.com/international/archive/2011/07/is-your-cell-phone-fueling-civil-war-in-congo/241663.

15. Hayden Cooper, "Factory Collapse a 'Wake-Up Call' for Fashion Industry," *ABC News*, https://www.abc.net.au/news/2013-04-30/bangladesh-building-collapse-fashion-industry/4661162.

16. Martin Luther King Jr., "Letter from the Birmingham Jail," *King Institute*, https://kinginstitute.stanford.edu/king-papers/documents/letter-birmingham-jail.

17. Dylan Thomas, "Do Not Go Gentle Into That Good Night," *Poem*.

Chapter 3:

FRAMEWORK

---

*"I worry we, like Pontius Pilate, are too quick
to wash our hands."*
- Dorena Williamson

In his article, "Isn't it Time for a New Mission Story?" activist and author Craig Greenfield makes a startling observation about missionary work among Buddhist cultures. "[U]nder Buddhism," Craig asserts, "for a god to 'love the world' would be shameful and strange. Love implies attachment. According to Buddha's Four Noble Truths, attachment to things causes sin. Buddhist religion teaches you to detach, not attach or love, in order to escape reincarnation and enter Nirvana. So, whoever this god is that is being described as 'loving,' to a... Buddhist, he is full of unholy passion and therefore must be a sinner."[1]

Craig's overall point is very simple: the best person to reach a Buddhist is a local who has grown up under the same worldview. Western missionaries often think of themselves as the enlightened saviors coming to reveal the beauty of the gospel; but because they cannot contextualize to the deeply entrenched nuances of the region, they end up proclaiming a strange belief filled with foreign concepts that make little sense to the people they are reaching.

As a pastor who is also a lifelong Adventist, the love of God is the most beautiful and profound truth I have to talk about. I have said it multiple times in sermons as well–I have nothing more profound to declare to you than this one thing: that God loves you. Consequently, Craig's article took a stab at the one thing I feel is the foundation of all Christian thought and theology. To think that there is a group of people out there for whom the love of God is repulsive rather than attractive is beyond me. Which means, I probably wouldn't make a very good missionary among the Buddhists.

The same issue applies in our Western context as well. While Western countries once enjoyed a majority Christian population, this is no longer the case.[2] More and more people increasingly identify as "nones," meaning, they have no religious affiliation or even background.[3] And yet, Adventists continue to preach the gospel today the way we did in the 1950s. We use the same frameworks, examples, explanations, and emphasize the same points. But what if the world has changed so much that, like a Buddhist, a traditional approach to the gospel can come across just as foreign in our emerging secular milieu?

Now, of course, this is an uncomfortable realization. For many of us–especially Adventists–a background in legalism, fundamentalism, and behaviorism has given us the kind of baggage that responds most meaningfully to a traditional approach to the gospel. We love to talk about grace, the free gift of justification, and we emphasize–until we are blue in the face–that salvation is free, free, free! And this is a message we fundamentally adore. After decades of living under the bondage of Last Generation Theology and its explicit perfectionistic soteriology, most of us find great joy and satisfaction in the works of Morris Venden, George R. Knight, Bill Liversidge, Martin Weber, and Marvin Moore. Their writings, frameworks, and explanations have been immensely liberating to so many of us suffocating under the burden of legalism.

However, what if I told you that this same gospel of free grace that we so passionately love makes very little sense to emerging secular culture? What if I told you that we actually have to change our approach entirely because this perspective, while intensely meaningful for us, is essentially boring to the secular man? Would you believe me? I hope so.

Some years ago, I was leading a Bible study at a cafe in my city. At the table were two Adventists and one secular friend. We dove into the gospel and, as the conversation progressed, it became dominated by the two Adventists. They were both suffering under the burden of false teachings like perfectionism and needed gospel relief. I took the time to explain it to them, but the questions just kept coming. There was so much mess to clear out that it was going to take some time. About a half-hour into the conversation, I glanced over at the secular guy as he let off a giant yawn, his eyes glazed over. He was bored.

I snapped back to reality and realized I was spending so much time undoing legalism for the Adventists, that the secular guy was lost. He couldn't understand what was so complicated. Jesus died for our sins and offers us eternal life free of charge. What's there not to get? Can we move on now?

The secular man had no concept of legalism, perfectionism, fundamentalism, or any of that baggage Adventists often bring to the table. Consequently, the gospel approach that we often take to relieve a person of those burdens made little sense to him. In fact, he found it utterly meaningless. I was reminded that the gospel must be reframed entirely for emerging secular culture or else, we risk preaching a message that they simply cannot grasp. In this chapter, I want to highlight three perspectives that are common in gospel presentations that make no sense to secular thinkers. In the next chapter, I will offer a framework that has been successful in my local context.

Saved by Grace, Not Works

As I already mentioned above, secular people don't have the theological baggage Adventists tend to have. As a result, the gospel perspective on being saved by grace and not works is one that we like to emphasize over and over again. However, without the background of trying to earn God's love or salvation, most secular people I have studied with find the whole idea of salvation as a gift really easy to grasp. I have never had a mountain of follow-up questions related to the free gift of salvation. So long as you have approached the conversation the right way, the entire concept makes good sense, and they are happy to move on rather quickly.

Some might push back and say that this perspective is so central to the gospel that it needs to be pushed as much as possible. Now, I do agree that we need to make sure it's clear. Legalism is something that is very natural to the human heart. All of us are trying to be saved by our own works. For the religious person, that may take the form of religious piety. For the secular person, it may take the form of self-help books, activism, and behavior modification.

However, the difference is that for a secular individual, salvation is about making this world a better place, and their works are about the transformation of society for a more just and equitable future. Thus, legalism in the secular sense is nowhere near the same as legalism in a religious sense. There is no anxiety about whether or not your works are good enough to grant you eternal life. The absolute best a secular person can hope for is that their works are good enough to grant the next generation a platform to continue to thrive, and this doesn't appear to have the same level of existential impact that religious legalism brings with it.

In religious legalism, there is concern over one's eternal state that is not present in secular thought. You worry if your works are good enough to earn you entry into heaven. You worry if you have confessed, repented, or behaved well enough by obedience to God's laws and standards. If you haven't, the threat of eternal damnation and death torments you. Even if you don't believe in eternal torment, you still know that you are missing out on eternal bliss because you couldn't get your act together on earth.

These variables are present not just in the experience of many conservative Adventists, but in the New Testament environment where Jesus had just abolished the Old Covenant. Greek converts were being harassed by Judaizers who wanted to bring them under the terms of the Old Covenant. Likewise, Hebrew believers had to learn to let go of the Old Covenant restrictions, as well as the extra burdens the Pharisees had been imposing on them. They had to learn to see God with new eyes by abandoning the eyes of legalism and embracing the eyes of love. Thus, Paul's letters—specifically Romans and Colossians—are of immense value to anyone whose religious experience has been damaged by these law-centered perspectives.

At the risk of being annoying, allow me to repeat once more—the contemporary secular mind is not steeped in this kind of atmosphere. Therefore, any gospel approach that leans exclusively or primarily on the "saved by grace, not works" motif is bound to fly over their heads every time. However, this does not mean that we ought to ignore this truth because it certainly is at the heart of the gospel. It simply means that we need to reframe the way in which we bring it up and explain it. But before we can do this, we first need to identify another perspective that secular thinkers struggle to wrap their heads around: sin.

Saved from Sin

For Christians of all stripes, the primary means by which we introduce the gospel is by presenting a problem and a solution. The problem we introduce is sin and, of course, the solution is Jesus. Some have described it as introducing the disease before you introduce the cure. As effective as this approach has been, its day is over. To the secular mind—particularly Millennials and Zeds—it sounds no different from the marketing sales pitches they hear almost every day of their social-media-bombarded lives.

Previous generations were not as overwhelmed with marketing as younger generations (described as "literally attached to smartphones, tablets, and laptops"[4]). This means that younger generations can spot a sales pitch a mile away, and the truth is, they aren't interested.[5] Virtually every young person today knows that the way you sell a product is by solving a problem (or creating one if there isn't any). Once the problem has been identified or manufactured, you can then turn around and offer your unique solution. For Christianity, the problem is sin, and the solution is Jesus. How convenient.

Perhaps this is why emerging generations prefer New Age and Buddhist perspectives when it comes to spiritual things. There is no sales pitch in these approaches to life. There is a recognition of the human soul, its emptiness and need, and these systems emerge as non-coercive, personalized, and malleable pathways through the angst. Unlike Christianity, with its clearly defined formulas, Buddhism, for example, allows the practitioner to determine his own path. A traditional Christian might see this as evidence that the secular man just wants to do his own thing and be in control of his own life. But the more astute student of the culture will see this as evidence that the secular man is searching for meaning, not sales pitches drowning in manipulative marketing techniques packaged in Christian jargon.

This is why, in the segments on the nature of man and

absurdity, I suggested that we need to begin the conversation in Genesis 1, not Genesis 3. Our story to humanity must begin at the Imago Dei, not the fall. We need to celebrate and uplift the beauty of the human being rather than profit off its moral fall—a perspective that is also difficult to comprehend in our mostly relativist society. Thus, while it is true that we are saved from sin, the very idea of being saved from sin needs to be reframed to speak more meaningfully to the secular language of being.

Once Saved Always Saved

Adventists don't believe in once saved always saved (OSAS). However, a long history of legalism has left many of us sympathizing with the concept. As a result, over the years, I have met many Adventists—including pastors—who want to emphasize eternal security so much that they end up centimeters away from a once saved always saved theology. Once again, this is a perspective that might appear attractive within a religio-centric community trying to undo the damage of legalism within its midst. But from a secular perspective, OSAS is repulsive. The fact that Adventists don't believe it makes little difference because most secular people do not have the theological insight to differentiate the nuances. If we are emphasizing eternal security over against anything else, as far as the secular man is concerned, we are teaching OSAS.

But why is OSAS so repulsive to the culture? The reason is quite simple. From the outside looking in, the secular man sees a church full of people who gather on the weekend to worship God. They sing songs, quote verses, and preach sermons about the free gift of salvation and how, once you have it, you can't lose it. There are smiles everywhere, upbeat music to celebrate the good news, and an altar call inviting people to receive this amazing gift. Isn't God the best?

But secular individuals see more than this. They see a group of people who sing about how "forever-forgiven" they are while at the same time perpetuating suffering on the earth. They are indifferent to racial disparity, gender discrimination, environmental issues, and coercive interpersonal dynamics. In that audience, thanking God for his forever-forgiveness, are abusive husbands who hit their wives the night before, racists, sexists, bigots, and liars. And even among those who are not actively perpetuating suffering, there is an even greater number who don't really care. But hey, they are forever-forgiven, so God is the best, right?

This tension is amplified in our contemporary political milieu. At the time of this writing, Donald Trump has become president for the second time. And a large part—if not the largest—of his support base are evangelical Christians, some of whom advocate for a future in which the church controls the state. From the outside looking in, evangelicalism has sold itself out for power. But, they are forever-saved, right?

Now, lest you be tempted to think that the secular person is being unfair in her or his assessment, let us recall the medieval church with its history of bloodshed, the magisterial Protestant reformers with their history of oppression and anti-Semitism. Let us not forget that it was the church that defended slavery in the American South, held its tongue during apartheid in South Africa, and complied with the unjust policies of the Nazi regime in Germany. It is also the church that now fights to regain political power in the USA, attempts to legislate its morality over the consciences of others, and has developed theological frameworks that have justified male dominance over women[6] and the mistreatment of immigrants.[7] But hey, we are forever-forgiven, so God is the best, right?

Thus, to the secular man, the good news that we so passionately espouse—that if you pray a prayer of surrender to Jesus you have a free ride to heaven no matter what—sounds like the most repulsive, unjust religious loophole that has ever existed. Add to this the fact that Christians say you can't go to heaven unless you receive Jesus as your personal savior, and you are left with a confusing spectacle in which an abusive and racist church elder can go to heaven because he has his "forever-forgiven" ticket while the kind and altruistic atheist is going to hell. This tension over grace and forgiveness was most clearly exhibited in the case of Brandt Jean's graceful response to his brother's (Botham Jean) killer. While many responded with admiration, many others were critical of this "forgiveness" that perpetuates cycles of suffering by releasing perpetrators from justice. Thus, Christian writer Dorena Williamson published a reaction in Christianity Today titled, "Botham Jean's Brother's Offer of Forgiveness Went Viral. His Mother's Calls for Justice Should Too"—a piece in which Williamson urged the church to not "[d]istort the gospel" by elevating forgiveness over justice.[8] Her call was eloquently summarized when she wrote:

Forgiveness, we know, comes from the cross. But

there is no resurrection without the horror of crucifixion. I fear we have softened the sacrifice of Jesus because we dare not linger on the bloody and gruesome body of a man tortured by the brutal law of the land, joined with a religious order. I worry we, like Pontius Pilate, are too quick to wash our hands.[9]

These three challenges to contemporary gospel proclamation demand a reframing of the good news. But reframing has always been in the DNA of Christ's evangelistic method. To a Jewish teacher he declared, "you must be born again" as a way of pushing back against the notion that Abrahamic birth was enough for entry to eternity. To a Samaritan woman he said, "I am the living water." And to a rich young ruler he said, "Sell all that you have and come follow me." Adapting the gospel to speak to the lived anxieties of your audience is not a modern invention in the face of mounting incredulity. It is at the very core of how God has always communicated with humanity.

And as our contemporary, meta-modern age steps aside to welcome the post-human era, this need will amplify all the more. What will that coming age look like? What will the new anxieties be? How can we adapt to articulate the gospel in a world governed by AI, humanoids, and quantum computing?

The honest truth is, no one fully knows. All we have are predictions that may or may not come true. But the reason why it's so hard to grasp is because we simply cannot fathom what a world in which AI surpasses human intelligence will look like. Which is why it's so important as missional believers to master the art of adapting our message here and now. If we develop our adaptive quotients, we will possess the skill to contextualize no matter what is happening around us. And it's a lot easier to develop those skills in a world we can still fathom, rather than to try and do it in a chaotic age which will be, by definition, undefinable.

In the next chapter, I am going to share a framework that is more meaningful in sharing the gospel with secular culture of today. But for now, I hope you can get an appreciation for why the approaches we are often passionate about may sound foreign and repulsive to the culture while being beautiful and attractive to us. If we wish to make a meaningful connection with the secular world, we must expand our approach to the gospel in a way that interacts more meaningfully with their values, priorities, and language of being. And as we do so, prepare ourselves for the changes that are soon to "break upon the world as an overwhelming surprise."[10]

———

Notes.

1. Craig Greenfield, "Isn't it Time for a New Mission Story?" in *Blog*,
https://www.craiggreenfield.com/blog/francischanmission ary

2. Pew Research, "In U.S., Decline of Christianity Continues at Rapid Pace," in *Pew Forum*,
https://www.pewforum.org/2019/10/17/in-u-s-decline-of-

christianity-continues-at-rapid-pace

3. Michael Lipka, "A closer look at America's rapidly growing religious 'nones,'" in *Pew Research Center*, https://www.pewresearch.org/fact-tank/2015/05/13/a-closer-look-at-americas-rapidly-growing-religious-nones

4. Daniel Newman, "Research Shows Millennials Don't Respond To Ads," in *Forbes*, https://www.forbes.com/sites/danielnewman/2015/04/28/research-shows-millennials-dont-respond-to-ads/#5ff04e965dcb

5. Tim Parker, "6 Ways to Sell to Millennials," in *Business Know-How*, https://www.businessknowhow.com/marketing/selltomillennials.htm

6. Michelle Boorstein, "Amid a Southern Baptist scandal, some evangelical women say the Bible's gender roles are being distorted to promote sexism," in *The Washington Post*, https://www.washingtonpost.com/news/acts-of-faith/wp/2018/05/22/amid-a-southern-baptist-scandal-some-evangelical-women-say-the-bibles-gender-roles-are-being-distorted-to-promote-sexism

7. Tara Isabella Burton, "The Bible says to welcome immigrants. So why don't white evangelicals?" in *Vox*, https://www.vox.com/2018/10/30/18035336/white-evangelicals-immigration-nationalism-christianity-refugee-honduras-migrant

8. Dorena Williamson, "Botham Jean's Brother's Offer of Forgiveness Went Viral. His Mother's Calls for Justice Should Too," in *Christianity Today*, https://www.christianitytoday.com/ct/2019/october-web-only/botham-jean-forgiveness-amber-guyger.html

9. Ibid.

10. Ellen G. White, *Maranatha: The Lord Is Coming* (Washington, D.C.: Review and Herald Publishing Association, 1976), p. 159.

Chapter 4:

REVERSAL

"We can and should eradicate aging as a cause of death, use technology to augment our bodies and minds, and merge with machines—remaking ourselves, finally, in the image of our own higher ideals."
- Mark O'Connell

In the previous chapter, we saw how traditional frameworks for explaining the gospel are no longer effective in our emerging post-Christian society. First, we saw that Christianity's heavy focus on salvation by grace and not works, while alleviating to the person steeped in legalism, barely registers with the mind of the secular thinker. This is a difficult concept for many Protestants to accept because our entire approach to the gospel is historically rooted in the unconditional gift of justification.

Our roots begin with Martin Luther, who, after decades of attempting to gain his own salvation, discovered the promise that "the just shall live by faith" (Rom. 1:17), that "by the works of the law shall no flesh be justified" (Rom. 3:20), and that salvation is "not of works, lest any man should boast" (Eph. 2:9). Thus, justification by faith became the center of Luther's theological proclamation to the degree that he could say, "Every week I preach justification by faith to my people, because every week they forget it."[1]

After Luther came Calvin, whose life's work centered on demonstrating that man can do nothing to be saved. Jacobus Arminius, George Whitfield, and John Wesley all fought to emphasize the same truth. While not as popular a reformer, perhaps few stated it as clearly as the English evangelical clergyman Charles Simeon when he said:

> Justification by faith alone is the hinge upon which the whole of Christianity turns.[2]

Thus, the Protestant psyche is deeply rooted in proclaiming the free gift of justification and ensuring that listeners have a clear and healthy understanding of the relationship between justification and works.

However, the contemporary secular milieu is one that has never heard of Luther, Calvin, or Arminius. They are unfamiliar with the legalism of Rome, the asceticism of the monks, and the debates over justification and sanctification. They do not come from the world of the Hindu, whose salvation depends on either the way of works, the way of knowledge, or the way of devotion. They do not have the background of the Buddhist, who aims to progress through the five pathways in order to attain Nirvana. They have never lived under the pressure of the five pillars of Islam or the ceremonial laws of Judaism.

Therefore, a gospel heavy on grace versus works—while liberating and of great utility for the religious person who has ever lived to attain redemption through moral purity—is of little significance to the secular psyche that has never read a Bible, entered a church, or wondered if they are good enough to go to heaven.

In fact, the opposite is true. If there is any theological heavenward path in the secular mind, it simply revolves around being a good person, alleviating suffering, and living a life of equilibrium. There is no complicated formula. There is no devotion to a deity, no magical prayers, ritualistic expectations, or acts of piety. Just be human. A good one. Not perfect—just authentic—and that will suffice. Everything else is overcomplicated religious noise at best and manipulative ideology at worst, designed to exploit the weak in order to perpetuate religious institutions.

And what about heaven? Perhaps the self-described techno-spiritualist Matthew Hoffman captured the cultural mantra best:

> I'll act as much like Jesus taught as I can because I feel that's a great way to live. Will I get rewarded in Heaven? I don't care.[3]

To this simple view of reality, the message that we are not saved by how good we are but by faith in Jesus sounds like salvation by a formulaic ascent to a historical figure purported to be a deity. This, to the post-church world, seems like bad news, not good news, because it suggests that God doesn't value virtuous living but instead demands religious allegiance.

Likewise, when the Christian starts speaking of sin, the secular mind—steeped in moral relativism—wanders off.

The supposed irresistible beauty of eternal security is interpreted as a religious loophole easily exploited by perpetrators of individual and collective injustice and suffering. The perpetrator can now rest assured in his assurance of salvation, a theme he obsessively defends, while the people he hurt are left to pick up the pieces of a broken life—often so wounded that they are overcome by cynicism and reject all faith, an act which the same perpetrator now conveniently condemns.

In the end, the victim who never embraced the formula goes to eternal death, while the perpetrator, who got the golden ticket to heaven, gets to live forever in bliss.

To make matters worse, all traditional frameworks for explaining the gospel suffer from a fatal flaw. Regardless of how eloquent its presenter, one cannot seem to get away from the fact that, at the end of all our eloquence, the gospel appears to be reducible to a simple formula: "Follow me, or I'll kill you."

This, the secular person sees as the underlying oppressive nature of Christianity.

Leave behind all the talk of grace and love—for it is mere propaganda, a cleverly worded public relations campaign to beautify what is, in truth, a divine dictator bent on annihilating anyone who does not comply with his imposed demands.

Thus, grace is seen as a free gift offered to anyone who abandons their autonomy in order to embrace the religious ideals that God approves. Anyone who rejects this grace, he erases from existence—their voice and protest never to be heard again.

Could there ever be another narrative as oppressive and simultaneously romanticized as this?

I hope this summary helps close any gaps that might remain in the reader's understanding of how the secular mind interprets and relates to the good news. If the gospel is to make any sense, it must be reframed in a way that speaks meaningfully to the objections that our post-to-meta-modern transition is contending with.

In my particular context, I have found an approach that is helpful. It follows a progressive three-step pattern that revisits the concepts of the cosmic tear/vacuum, followed by the restoration of harmony, and concludes with what I refer to as the divine reorientation towards the highest possible good.

The Cosmic Tear, Revisited

We have already introduced the cosmic tear in our chapters on the Great Controversy. But here, in exploring the gospel, is where this concept becomes most useful. As I noted before, the culture finds words like *sin* questionable because the word itself has been abused by the church. We have judged others, condemned others, and accused others of sin so much that the mere mention of the term raises a person's defenses. Therefore, rather than getting hung up on a term that triggers negative reactions, I explore it from a different vantage point: the cosmic tear.

However, because the goal is to explore the gospel here, I zoom in a little more by focusing on how the cosmic tear exists within us—individually and collectively. That is, the tear that damaged the design of reality is not simply a problem *out there*; it is likewise a problem *in here*. I then ask the person I am discussing with what this inner tear means to them. How have they seen it manifested in their lives or the lives of others? At this point, the conversation often moves into themes like trauma, injustice, and relational wounds.

The cosmic tear as an inner reality simply means that every human being is born out of alignment with the original design of reality because that design is not currently operational in our dimension. As a result, we enter the world with an inner tear that predisposes us to perpetuate the tear in a diversity of ways. It's as if the cosmic tear leads to the inner tear, which results in a pantheon of relational tears. These smaller, repeated tears continually destabilize the environments we live in, and when thousands and millions of people are involved, we end up with social, systemic, and civil injustices that accelerate harm and suffering. But again, the problem is not *out there*. It is *in here,* in the human heart, where the tear resides and where the impulse of love has been replaced by the lust for self.

I have yet to meet one person who denies that they have been selfish in life. After exploring with them the beauty of humanity, the *Imago Dei,* and the original design of creation, I ask, *"What happened?"* It's no lie—our world is far from the paradise of Genesis 1-2. We then talk about Lucifer's rebellion and lay the foundation for the cosmic tear. Once clear, I move into the inner tear and its role in reauthoring us from other-centered love to self-centered drives.

"What would happen if your selfish patterns were multiplied the world over—would the world be a more beautiful place or a tenser place?" is the question I ask. Now granted, sometimes people struggle to judge themselves. So, I have also found it easier to admit my own self-centered tendencies and then ask them the same question with myself as the subject: *"If my selfish patterns were multiplied in every corner of the globe, would this be a more beautiful world or not?"* The answer is easily *no*.

My selfish patterns, multiplied in the world around me, would compound exponentially into more self-centeredness and, consequently, more suffering. At this point, I tell my fellow sojourner that my patterns of selfishness are already multiplied in the world around us. Those same patterns exist in every human being and lead to tension, violence, and injustice everywhere we go.

I then switch gears and ask, *"If God were to get rid of all the self-centered impulses in this world at noon today, what would happen to me?"* Well, one of two things. If God destroys all selfishness, either I will be destroyed with everyone else, or—if I live on—I will no longer be *me*, for I love my selfishness and am bound to it, even to the point of identity. I then ask, *"What about you?"*

In my experience, this question tends to be the *aha* moment that allows the post-Christian to see with clarity why God doesn't simply wipe out all the *bad people*. The truth is that evil is not a thing to contend with externally but internally. The problem is not merely *out there* with *those people* but *in here* with me. I am part of the collective web of humanity, and all of us are driven by the compulsion to place self above others.

Now, suppose there really are measurably good people on the earth. If God gets rid of the bad ones and leaves only the good ones, how long before those good people turn bad and start fighting each other? How long until their offspring go to war? How long until we end up exactly where we are today?

At this point, people often begin to grasp the idea that all of humanity—despite its beauty—is deeply flawed. Humanity is, as Simone de Beauvoir once said, *"weighted down by present events... bewildered before the darkness of the future, which is haunted by frightful specters, war, sickness, revolution, fascism, bolshevism."*[4]

To this reality, Beauvoir contends that man's greatest fear is that, in the face of this unavoidable unknown, he will be forced to recall the *"agonizing consciousness of himself."*[5] Thus, it is not too great a task to conclude that the social and humanitarian landscape of our globe is so steeped in injustice that all of us are tied in and unable to escape.

Therefore, if God is to restore the world back to its original beauty and harmony, how will he do it? If he is to restore me or you back to the image of love, how will he accomplish this? If humanity is ever to procure its greatest possible goodness—what writer Tarun Mittal referred to as the attainment of our *"massive potential"*[6]—liberated from the oppression of the impulse of self, how will this ever come to pass?

The Reversal of the Way of Self

This is where the gospel comes in. Jesus, who is God, came to our world to set us free from the oppressive regime of the self and restore us to the image of love, which we were originally designed to reflect. In this sense, the gospel isn't simply about me being *forever forgiven* but about my restoration. God is not justifying the unjust, the oppressor, the self-centered, and the abuser—granting them some free pass to heaven because they believe in Jesus—only to allow those same people to continue perpetuating suffering in their spheres of influence.

To the contrary, when God justifies the unjust, the very act brings with it a metamorphosis of being that begins a process of healing and restoration. The unjust become just. The oppressor becomes the liberator. The abuser becomes a defender. The self-centered become other-centered. Thus, the gospel has virtue—or utility—in that, through it, the way of self is reversed. As this reversal is exponentially perpetuated throughout the earth, a new kingdom emerges—a kingdom driven by the ethic of love rather than the impulse of self.

It was this kind of Christianity that the anti-Nazi theologian Dietrich Bonhoeffer referred to when he wrote:

> We are not to simply bandage the wounds of victims beneath the wheels of injustice; we are to drive a spoke into the wheel itself.[7]

But how is this possible? Well, this is the good news of

salvation. God became a man in the person of Jesus. As a man, he lived out love in a way no other human being ever has. Jesus was the perfect man. But notice, Jesus was not religious in any traditional sense of the term. He had his customs, yes, but beyond that, we cannot regard Jesus as religious in the way we often speak of religion.

Instead, what we find is that Jesus was *human*–human in the most authentic sense, human in the most complete and undeniable way. The biblical witness, then, seems more concerned with revealing his humanity than his religion because the biblical narrative is not about religion but about humanity. Jesus is part of that narrative–a divine call to return to our original design and finally become who we are in the fullest sense. Thus, the biblical call to salvation is not about being more religious but about being more human–a return to the *Imago Dei,* reflected most fully in the person of Jesus.

Does this mean we ignore justification or downplay the difference between grace and works? Of course not. Those foundations need to be clear, especially when we consider that we must not only introduce our community to the gospel but also inoculate it from false gospels that seek to bring them under the bondage of religion. Salvation, I am clear, is not *what Jesus did plus what I do.* It is the work of Jesus only.

Nevertheless, the gospel is itself a dance between heaven and earth. To the secular age–steeped in social justice and the pursuit of a just future for all–a gospel that offers a logic toward true restoration and justice is just as important as the promise that salvation is a gift from beginning to middle to end.

The Divine Reorientation Towards the Highest Possible Good

This perspective on the gospel helps solidify three things:

1. It solidifies the fallenness of humanity.

2. It solidifies the need for salvation to come from beyond.

3. It solidifies the need for salvation itself to have utility beyond the psychological relief of guilt.

All three of these elements are valued within secularism's language of being. When approached properly, the gospel can be presented point by point without ever straying from either the pillars of the good news itself or the value structure of contemporary secular culture.

While the secular world is not steeped in religious legalism, it is nevertheless steeped in its own version of self-redemption. Humankind today is attempting to redeem itself from annihilation through environmental reform—a call reflected best in Greta Thunberg's observation that our doom will only come to pass if *"we choose"*[8] to doom ourselves.

If that fails, humankind aims to save itself from extinction through space exploration—what Jeff Bezos referred to as going *"to space to save the earth."*[9] And if this fails, humanity aims to immortalize itself through the transhuman goal of fusing human with machine—what Mark O'Connell refers to as *"remaking ourselves, finally, in the image of our own higher ideals."*[10] In each case, the scenario is the same: humans are, via the medium of science, attempting to secure their own salvation.

To this, the gospel speaks beautifully because it reminds us that no matter what we do or where we go, we will always be teetering on the precipice of self-annihilation, for we are the perpetuators of our own suffering. Until the impulse of self is healed and a new world, filled with a new impulse, is born, there can be no true rest, no true atonement, no true salvation.

And this, the gospel promises by posturing that in Christ, the human heart can be reoriented to daily advance toward its highest possible good. That is, the gospel reorients us to live inwardly, act outwardly, and relate upwardly in a poetic pursuit of what it means to be a humanity created in the image of love. This poetic life is thus an outflow of being, bringing divine love into the terrestrial village in tangible, meaningful ways.

We will explore this reorientation in more detail in the next chapter.

———

Notes.

1. Jason Abott, "Faith Alone," in *Theological Review.*

2. Ibid.

3. Matthew Hoffman, "8 Reasons I Believe in God and Don't Care About Heaven," in *Personal Reflections on Spirituality*.

4. Farnam Street, "Simone de Beauvoir on The Ethics of Freedom," in *Philosophical Essays on Freedom and Responsibility*.

5. *ibid*.

6. Tarun Mittal, "To be is to be: Jean-Paul Sartre on Existentialism and Freedom," in *Existentialist Thought and the Human Condition*.

7. Holly Thompson, "#InContext: Dietrich Bonhoeffer," in *Historical Theologies in Context*.

8. KC Baker, "Greta Thunberg on Her Fight to Save the Planet – and Why Asperger's Is Her 'Superpower,'" in *Environmental Advocacy and Climate Change*.

9. Kelsey Piper, "The Case Against Colonizing Space to Save Humanity," in *Futurist Perspectives on Space and Society*.

10. The Guardian, "No Death and an Enhanced Life: Is the Future Transhuman?" in *Technological Evolution and Human Identity*.

Vol. 2

Chapter 5:
METAMORPHOSIS

"I grasped the meaning of the greatest secret that human poetry and human thought and belief have to impart: The salvation of man is through love and in love."
-Viktor E. Frankl

I recently purchased the Audible version of the classic work *Man's Search for Meaning* by Holocaust survivor and psychiatrist Viktor E. Frankl. In the first part of the book, Frankl unravels his own horrors as a prisoner at Auschwitz and Dachau. While he intentionally restrains himself from going into too much detail, he nevertheless takes the reader into the stark, miserable quagmire of life that he and his fellow prisoners had to endure.

Focusing on the less dramatic experiences, he slowly brings the reader into the death camps. Time almost stands still as the imagination wraps itself around each scene and detail–the insults, beatings, and humiliation; the frostbite, illness, and starvation. All of it builds up until, at last, the sky turns gray with ashes, and one is immersed in the wretchedness of the Nazi machine.

Frankl's intent, however, is not to linger on the horrors but to extract meaning from them. To this end, his narrative arc brings him to a central point in the book where he describes himself, in the midst of a dark and hopeless night, being swept away by his imagination and seeing his wife. The experience was profoundly romantic and existential. For there, surrounded by barbed wire and guard towers, Frankl managed to escape and speak to his beloved. The experience, he described, provided him with a much-needed respite from the angst.

However, it gave him something more—a glimpse at the mystery of redemption that many great theologians have failed to ascertain. Frankl describes this glimpse as the epiphanous realization that *"[t]he salvation of man"*—a subject that has given rise to countless religions, political systems, and philosophies—*"is through love and in love."*[1] This awakening gave Frankl the capacity to endure almost unimaginable horrors and survive to become the founder of logotherapy and the author of the bestselling aforementioned book.

There is much that can be said about Frankl, for a great deal of what he wrote is immersed in a poetic dance between suffering and hope. But for our purpose in this particular chapter, I want us to focus on the idea of love's redeeming power. Somehow, in the midst of his agony, a man who had no personal commitment to the depths of Christian eschatology was able to glimpse the true end of the tale. Whether he ever knew it or not, Frankl's realization took him right to the center of God's heart, where he discovered that salvation—whatever complexities it entails—can be reduced to the singularity of love.

Of course, Frankl did not see this in theological terms so much as in psychological and philosophical ones. To be fair, his entire perspective was focused on how he could, by being tethered to his beloved in soul, transcend absurdity and press through that which, in most circumstances, drained men's will to live. Nevertheless, this romantic conceptualization of redemption, I contend, is but a reflection—a grasping at the wind, if you will—of revelation's soteriological current.

In the previous chapters, we have explored this narrative with the question: how can we reframe soteriology to speak beyond religio-centric concerns and directly to the heart of the secular mind? We have seen that the journey cannot begin with the classic grace-versus-works mentality because it doesn't make much sense to a non-religious mind.

Rather, the journey must begin in a different sphere and speak directly to the value structure the listener already has. In my particular context, I have found that value structure, while secular indeed, is more holistically biblical than the frameworks we often employ. For deep in the secular language of being, there is a longing for meaning, for autonomy and self-determination, and most of all—for a kind of justice that is so inherently divine that the overwhelming flood of postmodern relativism has been unable to extinguish it.

From this starting place, we can explore the origin of sin as a cosmo-political ideology of self-advancement. This ideology led to war in heaven and then spread to the earth, where humanity, by embracing the way of self over love, chose to rebel against its Maker. The result of this rebellion is that humans perpetuate the Satanic political regime by replacing the centrality of God and love with the pursuit of self. And it is this pursuit, deeply embedded and seemingly irremovable, that drives the human narrative constantly toward empire and injustice.

But here is where things get curious. And I want to use an illustration here to make sense of it. When we talk about the cosmic tear that harmed the fabric of reality, we speak of something that has affected reality as a whole, yes, but also the very human spirit itself. However, we also speak of something that would not have been possible without human abdication.

I promised an illustration to make sense of this, so here it goes: Imagine a top-secret computer held in a government facility. This computer cannot be accessed by anyone except a specially trained engineer who alone has the passcode. This means that if a terrorist hacker wants to get into the computer to plant a virus, he can only do it one way—he must trick the engineer into letting him in. There is no other way. No backdoor access. He either goes through the engineer or not at all.

In many ways, this is what we see happening in Genesis. The satan introduced a virus into our cosmological reality. But to do so, he had to go through the engineers in charge of the system. If he could trick them and gain access through them, he could introduce his tear. In some mysterious way, Adam and Eve were the access points to the system. Satan had to go through them to gain full access to the governing code of reality. And once he had this, he could rewrite that code with his own. The earth became his to govern.

This is why, in a later story depicting beings from other worlds meeting with God (Job 1), Satan appears representing the earth. But his system is not stable. He complains that he can't fully build the code he wants because there is a glitch in the system—one man in whose heart the original code remains. One man who clings to Yahweh. But the satan accuses Yahweh of calculated generosity in order to secure Job's loyalty. If this munificent relationship were to be disrupted, Job's true colors would show, and he would curse God instead. In the end, however, Job remains loyal, demonstrating that the original code of reality lives on. And if it lives on, even in the slightest way, there is hope that it can one day be fully restored.

And this is really the point of the entire redemptive story. But if it is ever to take true shape—that is, if God is to restore humanity to its original design—a reversal of the way of self must be actuated in real-time and in real human flesh. This reversal is complex, but the gospel is given to us in the language of children so that we can grasp the enormity of the promise: that God became a man, lived out love in all its perfection, and restores *through love and in love* all who put their trust in him.

This, of course, does not negate the very real and important element of justification by faith—that our life of self-centered adulation is absolved, absorbed by the sin-bearer on the cross. Now, covered by his virtue, we can celebrate the beautifully outrageous proposition that God regards us as complete in him, even though we are yet incomplete.

Nevertheless, the secular mind—far removed from the burdens of legalism—does not need to linger there too long. For Paul assures us that we are counted as perfect while we are being made holy, and to the secular man, this process toward practical holiness is of insurmountable value.

And it is here that I enter into the final perspective introduced in the previous chapter, which I, borrowing from clinical psychologist Jordan Peterson, have come to refer to as *the divine reorientation towards the highest possible good.*

The Divine Reorientation Towards the Highest Possible Good

We are all familiar with the words attributed to Mahatma Gandhi who, in protest of the British occupation of India, once noted: *"I like your Christ, I do not like your Christians. You Christians are so unlike your Christ."*[2]

The comedian Bill Maher also once stated:

> *There's no greater role model, in my view, than Jesus Christ. It's just a shame that most of the people who follow him and call themselves Christian's act nothing like him.*[3]

There is a clear sense in the culture—a zeitgeist that recoils from the supposed good news of a salvation free of demands. We Christians seem to think it a good thing. The culture, not so much. The secular mind is immersed in a perpetual tension between meaning and meaninglessness and has, in some sense, learned to exhibit moral outrage despite its enslavement to moral relativism.

There is something within that is crying out for a better world, a better economy, better borders, better education, and better governance. The mind of the culture is drenched in the sweat of its own labor for a world where there is no slave, no inequality, no disparity, and no injustice—a mindset at odds with the evolutionary proposition that life is disinterested in our ideals and that the universe is fundamentally cold and unfair.

To this milieu, the happy Christians and their *"Receive Jesus, and all your sins will be forgiven, and you can go to heaven. It really is that simple and free"* message are, quite frankly, laughable. Heaven is not desired. Forgiveness is not sought after. Assurance is not pursued. Rather, what the culture is attempting to do is construct a new tomorrow—a future in which humanity has achieved a collective and inclusive good, perhaps even the highest good that can be imagined.

In light of this pursuit, a gospel that fails to interact with this metamorphosis of society—by opting instead to linger at the pacification of individual religious pathologies—is an irrelevant message at best. At worst, it is part of the problem. Thus, in my interaction with secular culture, I always emphasize what Scripture refers to as the *transformation* of being, in which one's entire life is reoriented after the divine heart (*the highest possible good*) and molded in its image with *"ever-increasing glory"* (2 Cor. 3:18). This experience, the biblical witness views as a holistic *"renewal of the mind"* (Rom. 12:2), in which the divine dwells in you (Acts 17:28, Gal. 2:20) and becomes a *"spring of living water"* flowing through the soul (John 4:14), cleansing the conscience (Heb. 9:14), and restoring in us the image of love lost at the Fall (1 John 4:8).

In short, the experience of salvation is one in which the reborn finds herself experiencing a divine reorientation toward the highest possible good, which is Jesus himself—who lived out love in human flesh and toward whom the biblical authors call us to pattern and orient our lives.

"Walk as he walked" (1 John 2:6), *"Follow in his steps"* (1 Pet. 2:21), *"Be imitators… of Christ"* (1 Cor. 11:1), *"Walk in love, as Christ loved us"* (Eph. 5:1-2), *"Put on the new self, created after the likeness of God"* (Eph. 4:24), *"Put on Christ"* (Gal. 3:27), *"Have this mind… which is yours in Christ"* (Phil. 2:5), *"Set your mind on the Spirit"* (Rom. 8:8), and so on and so forth.

This biblical theme—in which the rebirthed consciousness is beckoned toward a reorientation of being and conduct, aimed at and patterned after the character of Jesus, *the sum of all that is meant by "the highest possible good"*—is deeply embedded in what it means to be a believer and follower of Jesus. As such, the gospel is good news for more than the fact that I can enjoy individual assurance. It is good news because the gospel is the promise of restoration for the collective web of the human race. God is at work, drafting and crafting a new kingdom filled with people whose lives are oriented toward love—a community that celebrates autonomy, self-determination, and authenticity while turning their backs on the deceptive allure of self-centeredness and allowing the Spirit of God to restore them to the image of other-centered love.

A kingdom of everyday humans who have discovered what it truly means to be human—and who live that humanity out, not in convents and monasteries, but in the daily brokenness of society. A people who are *salt* sprinkled on culture, on neighborhoods, and on empire. A people whose lives, while far from perfect, are nevertheless trending toward a transcendent love that moves them to live not for self but for others, and in whom the image of Jesus is reflected authentically, even in their blemished being. A people who, in the words of the reformer John Wesley, daily enact *"the humble, gentle, patient love of God and our neighbor"* by allowing this love to *"[rule their] tempers, words, and actions."*[4]

A people who are glitches in the satan's simulation.

This perspective of the gospel is often ignored in favor of a *hyper-grace* framework that focuses more on the free gift than the true cost. This is partly due to centuries of Roman legalism, which—at least in the Adventist context—was repeated in the rise and dominance of *Last Generation Theology,* a legalistic and perfectionistic approach to salvation that has littered Adventist history with the tattered and shipwrecked souls of the sincere.

But my contention is that it is time we build something beautiful out of the rubble of our legalistic trauma by rediscovering the salvific narrative of Scripture—a story in which salvation rises from the individual to the collective, from the local to the universal, from inner peace to outward recreation.

For the truth is that, once reborn, we are indeed led by the divine to orient our lives after the highest possible good and, in the midst of that reorientation, live out the ethic of love in the grind and agony of traffic, business, and struggle. And in doing so, we usher in the kingdom of God by living out its principles while occupying the temporal empire of man.

What would it look like if we stepped away from a grace-versus-works framework and focused on a more holistic vision of salvation as the restoration of humanity? Would our gospel not then speak meaningfully to humanitarian disparity, justice, and the reversal of suffering? Would our people not be moved to get over this obsession with personal assurance and realize that to follow Jesus means to think less of self, less of religion, less of laws—and more of love, *the highest love, which is Christ himself?*

Would our churches not mobilize to become epicenters of God's movement—spaces of healing and redemption in our communities? Would our evangelism not shift from informational models to more relational and missional approaches? Would our entire culture as a church not move from formulaic arguments over justification and sanctification and instead opt for a faith that is truly alive, meaningful, and felt in its sphere of influence? Would our faith not interact beautifully with the heart of a culture erroneously searching for a world beyond—by looking at the world within?

Søren Kierkegaard once said:

The highest and most beautiful things in life are not to be heard about, nor read about, nor seen but, if one will, are to be lived.[5]

And this is precisely what the culture awaits—a faith, a church, and a Jesus to be *lived,* in whom the highest dreams of humanity are fulfilled.

It is to this topic that we now turn. From the doctrine of the gospel to the doctrine of the church. But make no mistake, we are not yet done with the gospel. This is not a topical shift. As we begin to explore the church we must, of necessity, go deeper into the gospel and intensify our search for the synthesizing principle that brings all of these anxieties together into one gentle nucleus, offering our world a new horizon that none of our revolutions can ever approximate.

———

Notes.

1. Viktor E. Frankl, Man's Search for Meaning (Boston: Beacon Press, 2006).

2. Mahatma Gandhi, Gandhi Glimpsed Christ, Rejecting Christianity as a False Religion (New Delhi: Navjivan Trust, 1949).

3. Bill Maher, Quotes by Bill Maher (Los Angeles: HBO Real Time Archives, 2010).

4. John Wesley, A Plain Account of Christian Perfection (London: Epworth Press, 1766).

5. Søren Kierkegaard, "The Most Beautiful Things in Life Are to Be Lived": 9 Quotes from Christian Søren Kierkegaard (Copenhagen: Gyldendal, 1843).

Chapter 6:

NEO-BABEL

"It's unbearable to be able to look through that door and glimpse all the people you could have been and know that out of all of them, this is the one you became."
–Reichsmarshall John Smith

In the Amazon alternate-history web series *The Man in the High Castle*, a parallel universe is depicted in which the Axis powers—Italy, Germany, and Japan—have emerged as the victors in World War II. As a result, history unfolds quite differently, with the Nazis ruling the eastern United States, known as the *Greater Nazi Reich*, while the Empire of Japan rules the western half, renamed the *Japanese Pacific States*. Leading the Greater Nazi Reich is former U.S. Army soldier turned SS *Obergruppenführer* John Smith. As the series progresses, Smith climbs to the top of the Nazi party, becoming the *Reichsmarschall* of North America, answerable only to the *Führer* himself.

Without diving into the specifics of the show and its complicated plotlines, allow me to focus exclusively on *Reichsmarschall* John Smith. Throughout the show, it is difficult to identify Smith's ethical compass. Yes, he is a former American who now sits at the top of Nazi power, which ought to settle the issue. But at the same time, Smith exhibits redemptive qualities that revolve around his love for his family. In season one of the show, Smith assassinates a doctor who diagnoses his son with muscular dystrophy (a disease that renders one disposable in the Reich) in order to protect his son from being exposed and consequently euthanized. During the doctor's funeral, Smith provides a glimpse into his character when he says:

> A man is only ever as strong as the people around him—the community he serves and the family he swore to protect. Whatever strength he has, he draws from them. And for them, he must be prepared to give everything—his life for his blood—or else everything he has done has been for nothing. He is nothing.

This familial love constantly depicts Smith wrestling with the ethics of the Nazi empire—ethics that, despite his tireless efforts, eventually lead to the state-sanctioned termination of his only son. From this point in the series, it appears that Smith may actually be on the verge of recanting his allegiance to the Reich. However, in the end, Smith doubles down on his allegiance to evil and opts to perpetuate the injustice and oppression of the Nazi regime, thus opening the door to his own catastrophic end.

In the final episode of the series, Smith prepares to invade the western states and is confronted by his wife, Helen.

> "I've seen the plans," she says, referring to a new initiative of concentration camps on the West Coast. "How did we get here?" she presses. "You and me—how did we get here? And this thing that we have been a part of—it is a crime."

Smith's reply is cold and emotionless. *"I know."*

"It has to stop," Helen asserts.

Smith's breaths come heavy. He feels the tension of the moment. But in the midst of that tension, all he can afford to offer is a dead stare, followed by the hoarse whisper: *"I don't know how."*

What Smith is referring to is both profound and tragic. The man who once fought against the Nazis has, for so long, acted only in the interest of self-preservation that he has become one of them. It began with embracing the Reich in order to provide for his newborn son in the wake of a defeated American government. It led, little by little, to the once-good man becoming a part of the injustice and oppression of the Fascist *Wehrmacht*. Somewhere along the way, Smith lost himself and became entangled in a web of institutional injustice so complex and multifaceted that, in the end, he finds himself unable to escape the chain of events of his own making. His character has been molded in one direction, and even in the realization of his crime, he cannot walk away.

What we see before us, depicted in the life of this fictional *Reichsmarschall*, is that our decisions can entangle us in a web so strong—or place us in a maze so vast—that by all human capacity, we are unable to see a way out. And in many ways, this entanglement of being is what the culture today is contending with. There is such a vast and overwhelming array of ideas, counter-ideas, ethics and non-ethics, religions, and philosophies. These, coupled with the way in which a man conducts himself in the world—

all of his decisions, all of his lies, all of his cover-ups, all of his pursuits, all of his vices and patterns, all of his deeds done and left undone—are sprinkled with the acts of others, the influence of a fallen world impacting their sense of direction and passion. Media and family, school and literature, films and traditions, government, and anarchy— all of it, undergirded by his own predilections, pathologies, and genetics—leads every human being, eventually, to a point of entanglement too vast to contend with.

Is it any wonder, then, that amusements appeal so much to our hearts? Is it not obvious how the duties of life can drown us while promising to deliver us from the discomfort? Is it not clear how the promise of the next spiritual guru, with his path to freedom and inner peace, would attract the soul? Amusements, duties, and transcendence are the ways the culture chooses to navigate the web and—at last—find some semblance of meaning and peace in their lives. But in the end, as I have contended throughout this series, these systems of navigation crash, and the man is left to confront the web of insanity that entangles him, with no one to show him the way.

Purpose of the Church: Unraveling the Pathway Back to God

And it is to this end that God did not simply send Jesus to be our Savior—he also founded the church. The church, as Ellen White puts it, *"is God's appointed agency for the salvation of men."*[1] It has the purpose of carrying *"the gospel to the world"* and is a living and breathing community in which *"the final and full display of the love of*

God" can be seen and experienced.

To put it differently, the church is a living community in which the entangled soul of the culture can find its way back to the heart of God and experience redemption. The church, then, has a beautiful mission: to unravel the pathway to the heart of God and help lead the lost through the web of confusion and the maze of perplexity back to the Father. This is the church's mission.

The Church's Failure: From Maze to Maze

However, one dark stain damages the beauty of the church's mission: its failure. When I look around at the state of the church today, it is not a beautiful community leading the entangled soul to freedom and simplicity in Christ, but rather an entangled community itself. The church today is ensnared in its own web of self-perpetuation and religiosity. Thus, we add to the confusion of a wandering culture by placing before them demands and hoops through which they must jump in order to arrive at God.

Our message is not *"Find freedom from the web and the maze"* but rather *"Join our maze instead."* We move people from one state of confusion to another—from Babel to Babel. No longer is the church actively fulfilling its calling to provide a clear pathway toward God. Instead, we have settled for providing a pathway littered with obstacles of our own making.

We tell them:

Do you want to follow God? Wonderful. Now don't wear this, don't eat that, come to church this way, and don't worship like that. Make sure you stop listening to that music and listen to this one instead. Here's the best Bible translation around—it's written in ancient English, and most can hardly understand it, but you'll be fine—the Spirit will help you. And by the way, stay away from those churches, don't listen to those preachers, and don't read those books. If you're single, allow us to introduce you to purity culture, replete with its own set of endless laws on dating, marriage, and even dress. Let us bless you with the truth of our hyper-religious dogma so that you can be sure to live a life that is pleasing to God. Oh, and by the way, in the end of time, all the deceptions will lead many astray, and you can be one of them, so be careful. And Jesus? Yes, he is important, but don't forget—the little horn is what matters now. And grace? Yes, that's okay. Just make sure you keep the law. And if the laws in Scripture are not enough, here's a mountain of books written by our prophet with thousands more. Good luck. See you at church next Sabbath. Don't forget to wear a tie.

The above paragraph is certainly a caricature, but it is not inaccurate. Our church is sadly inundated with this mentality. Some manage to pace their demands on seekers by recognizing that people have to grow slowly, but the drive to make the new believer just like themselves never goes away. They might have enough civility not to overwhelm them, but the tension is always there—and you can feel it when you walk through the doors on Sabbath morning.

The church has sadly become as confused as the world, loaded down with the burden of its own institutional self-protection and drowning in its ideological preservationism. It can no longer interact with the culture in a significant way—leading it from confusion to clarity, from perplexity to simplicity, from Babylon to Jerusalem. Pastors know it. Administrators know it. But if you tell any of us that it must stop, our words will sadly echo the despondency of *Reichsmarschall* Smith—*"We don't know how."*

In this sense, we ourselves are blind—lost in our own maze—and yet, our evangelism gives the impression that we are here to guide others out of the maze. But what sense is there in guiding others out of a maze if we ourselves are entangled? In the end, we will only succeed at getting the culture to swap mazes—nothing more. And it is because of this ever-present reality that today the culture opts to seek God outside of the church and away from Christians.

Christians, they perceive, are trapped in the webs of institutional judgmentalism. They perpetuate the abuse of women and the forced legislation of morality while attending their services, smiles plastered across their faces as they sing of how forgiven they are. And if you want to join them, there is a mountain of complexity that will then be added to your life. *And my life is already complicated enough—so no, thank you. I'll construct my own religion, read my own books, and attend a few Tony Robbins and Deepak Chopra seminars to get some guidance. But overall, I'd rather do this on my own.*

Who can blame them?

The Tower of Babel, 2.0 (AKA, Neo-Babel)

One of the most significant books I have read in the last decade is Carl Teichrib's *Game of Gods: The Temple of Man and the Age of Re-Enchantment*. In this book, Teichrib, a missional Christian who runs a tent *"to the unknown God"* at the *Burning Man* annual festivals, argues that the culture has moved from a disenchanted modernism to a re-enchanted era with the goal of finishing the Tower of Babel (metaphorically speaking). This tower is man's new temple—man's self-redemption—and the exaltation of human potential as the ultimate divine.

Teichrib meticulously traces the tendrils of esoteric spirituality, globalist ideologies, and postmodern mysticism, revealing how they weave together into a bricolage of collective transcendence—one that bypasses the need for Christ. The book is unsettling in its implications, not because it sensationalizes, but because it soberly documents a shift that many believers sense but struggle to articulate.

We are witnessing a world where ancient pagan ideals, once buried under the weight of modern skepticism, are being resurrected—not in their original forms, but through a fusion of technology, psychology, and mysticism. The self has become the altar, personal enlightenment the liturgy, and universal unity the creed. It is a re-enchantment that promises freedom but often leads to deeper entrapment—a gospel of self-salvation that echoes Eden's oldest whisper: *"You shall be as God."*

And yet, for all its allure, this grand reconstruction is as fragile as Babel itself. The temporal human frame cannot bear the burden of ultimate meaning. And yet, it trudges onward, scratching in the dark, searching for something that will work. Technological revolutions in quantum computing, AI, and bio-mechatronics seem to offer the missing link many are searching for.

But if there is one area that Teichrib fails to address, it is this: the church today has become so insular, so judgmental, so oppressive that the soul of a longing culture cannot consider it. Yes, Christ will always be countercultural and, as such, a threat to imperial and social normativity's. But this is not why the church finds itself at odds with the culture today. The tension has less to do with the anti-conformal nature of Christ and more to do with the way in which the church mirrors empire and perpetuates its patterns of exclusion and contention.

And to that end—where is the culture to turn in its search for meaning? Where will it go in its pursuit of justice and compassion? Can it turn to the church with its lust for power? Can it turn to the church with its cruelty toward LGBTQIA+ communities? Can it turn to the church with its patriarchal structures, its abuse coverups, its financial exploitations, and its desire to dominate?

If we were to wind back the clock just 50-100 years, we could ask: *Could the culture turn to the church with its support of apartheid in South Africa? With its endorsement of the Nazi party in Germany? With its compliance with Jim Crow in America?* In fact, forget compliance—it led the way! In defending slavery. In the fight for segregation. In the struggle over keeping America *pure* from the "*savagery of the Black man",* the church was not merely complicit, it was the architect of the storm.

Where does a longing soul turn when the church is nowhere to be found—and that which we call the church is but a rearticulation of empire, appropriating Bible verses and religious rituals in order to appear sublime, when in reality, it is but an extension of the state with its temporal aspirations for more power, more wealth, and more control?

Our Collective Laodicea

The Man in the High Castle ends tragically. A despondent *Reichsmarschall* Smith speaks to the show's main protagonist, Juliana Crain. He and Crain have been able to travel to parallel universes and see other versions of themselves in worlds where the Nazis lost the war.

"It's unbearable," Smith begins, as he sits on the edge of a cliff following the death of his wife. *"It's unbearable to be able to look through that door and glimpse all the people you could have been—and know that out of all of them, this is the one you became."*

A single, self-inflicted gunshot brings an end to the man who—to all onlookers—had ample opportunity to take a different course. How tragic that, in the name of convenience and comfort, Smith lost his own soul. In a sense, he was dead long before he pulled the trigger.

As we contend with the challenges of reaching the secular

world, I wonder if Smith is as much a mirror for the church as he is for the culture.

Look around us. *What have we become?* How foreign are we to the original purpose for which we were called?

The church today is a performance, a show, a museum. We use it for our own self-gain. We use it to preserve our traditions, to conserve our customs and dogmas. The church today is a monument of a bygone era, and we like it that way. It has lost its way–its soul–in the pursuit of comfort and convenience. But you better not change it.

Like Smith, we all know something is wrong, but we don't know how to fix it, so we just go along. We go along with organizing programs for the sake of programs, events for the sake of events. We preach, we sing, we repeat. The world around us drowns in its confusion, longs for redemption, and builds its new temple–but when (a very rare when) they turn to us for insight, we repel them with our own insipidness.

And the worst part? So many of us seem to be *okay* with it.

In the next chapter, I will share a simple process by which I aim to redesign local churches to recapture their essence and purpose. Because the truth is, when it comes to the doctrine of the church, it's not merely *what we say* that is problematic in our evangelistic endeavors–it's *what we do* and *fail to do.*

It's time we did something different.

It's time we embodied the synthesis.

Notes

1. Ellen G. White, *Acts of the Apostles* (Mountain View, CA: Pacific Press, 1911), p. 9.

Chapter 7:

MOBILITY KILL

"Teach me, O God... to breathe deeply in faith."
—Soren Kierkegaard

Imagine a scenario with me. You are an Allied lieutenant during World War II. Your platoon is part of an assault on France aimed at liberating the country from its German occupiers. As the raid begins, you find yourself with a small company of stranded paratroopers. Radio checks indicate you are miles away from the nearest Allied reinforcements, and the Germans are pushing back. You know there is no way you will survive alone, so you direct your troops to carefully make their way toward the Allies.

As you maneuver under the cover of darkness, you discover that your way is blocked by an enemy patrol. Your platoon prepares for a surprise attack, but then a frightening sound fills the air. It's the sound of thick steel tracks crushing the ground beneath them. You glance toward the German troops just ahead, and your worst fears are confirmed—a Panzer tank—arguably the most powerful mechanized weapon in the Reich's arsenal—has just entered the scene.

Your platoon sergeant approaches with an alternative plan.

You both know there is no way you can engage the tank in combat. Sitting atop the tank is a long-barrel 75 mm cannon joined by two fully automatic machine guns. Directly underneath them is a layer of armor so thick your bullets and explosives will be unable to penetrate it. And then, of course, the metal tracks beneath the tank enable it to move across the roughest terrain. The chances of sneaking past without being spotted are slim, and if you are discovered, that Panzer guarantees most of you won't live to tell the story.

There is only one possible scenario in which you and your men can make it past this insurmountable roadblock and push ahead to friendly territory. Your platoon sergeant unravels the wild plan. "Somehow," he says, "that tank has to be disabled. We cannot destroy a Panzer—we don't have the firepower—but if we render it inoperable, we can outmaneuver it and push ahead."

Your platoon sergeant gathers all the explosives in the team's possession. "Set this up where the tank will pass and detonate it," he says. "It won't destroy the tank, but it will destroy the tracks that enable it to move. If it can't move, it can't fight, and we can get out of here."

The above scenario is far from an imaginative game but a common occurrence during World War II referred to as a "mobility kill." Rather than destroying the tank, you destroy its mobility using landmines or other explosives. Of course, the tank is still dangerous and can cause lots of damage, but it can no longer complete its objective.

And this is precisely what Satan is doing to the church. The Adventist Church is like a tank. It has a top level with powerful spiritual warfare tools (resources, media, leadership, etc.) and a lower level with impenetrable armor (lawyers, administrators, policies, etc.). However, none of this is what enables the church to move. Like a real tank, the armor and weapons are not what make the tank effective. Rather, it is the tracks underneath. Likewise, the Adventist Church moves into the world via its tracks–the local church. It is the local church that moves the tank into action. Without the local church, the tank sits still and goes nowhere. With the local church, the tank is in motion.

Which means something very simple. If Satan wants to stop the Adventist movement, he doesn't need to destroy its weapons or attack its armor. That's too much work. All Satan has to do is execute a "mobility kill" by destroying the tracks (the local church). Once he has done this, the church itself is still intact and dangerous, but it can no longer complete its objective. With the tracks gone, the Adventist movement grinds to a halt, and the enemy outmaneuvers us on his way to seduce and distort the culture.

Look around. It's happening everywhere. Our church has remarkable resources, finances, and logistical capacity, but Adventism–especially in the West–is dying. It is not moving the way it should but is like a tank without tracks–it can still do some damage, but overall, the tank is useless. Satan hasn't had to destroy the conferences, unions, or divisions. He hasn't had to go after publishing houses or media ministries (although he certainly attacks those as well).

All he's had to do to stop Adventism's movement is render the local church inoperable. Demolish those with division, dissension, and fanaticism. Destabilize them with preservationism, legalism, and cynicism. Dismantle them with traditionalism, conservatism, and reactionism, and you end up with a church that runs hospitals, schools, bookstores, aged care centers, universities, satellite channels, and publishers yet remains–for all intents and purposes–completely irrelevant in the contemporary battlefield. It has stopped moving, stopped learning, stopped listening, stopped growing, stopped loving, and stopped serving because it has fallen victim to the enemy's guerrilla tactic designed to render us inoperable while leaving us otherwise intact.

The Danish philosopher and father of existentialism Søren Kierkegaard contended with this very tension in his day in what has been referred to as his "sustained attack on all of Christendom."[1] Kierkegaard's context was different in that he was combating the state religion, which he felt turned Christianity into "a mere fashionable tradition,"[2] but despite that contextual difference, the fundamental issues he protested are still alive today.

For Kierkegaard, true faith "was not a doctrine to be taught, but rather a life to be lived."[3] This living, active faith is something Kierkegaard increasingly felt was absent in the established church, which he regarded as neither biblical nor Christian. On the contrary, Kierkegaard described the church of his day as "a forgery, a falsification,"[4] which he contended was "brought about over the centuries, whereby Christianity has gradually become just the opposite of what it is in the New

Testament."[5]

Consequently, Christians had become "lazy in their religion,"[6] were merely "playing at Christianity,"[7] and lacked "unconditional religious commitment"–all of the building blocks for what can be regarded as "empty religion."[8] In the end, Kierkegaard felt the state of the church was a primary contributor to the condition of the age in which man had become indifferent to faith. Kierkegaard summarized this best in what can be metaphorically regarded as his eulogy of the faith when he surmised, "the human race has outgrown Christianity."[9]

As Adventists, we have historically regarded ourselves as heirs of the Reformation and, in some ways, the remaining movement that carries that torch to the end of history. And while this may be true of the message we proclaim, it is not difficult to see that our churches are, to borrow from Kierkegaard, spiritually "empty." Rather than active communities of faith that live out the gospel in tangible, meaningful ways, our churches tend to be established clubs with preset rules and rituals that we mindlessly repeat week after week with very little thought given to how any of this translates into the absurdity of life.

Consequently, we become just another institutional drum that produces lazy religion, conditional religious commitment, and empty faith. And as we conduct ourselves this way in the world, we give the culture every reason to regard us with indifference and to bypass the church as though it is a relic of an age long past. This has been Satan's tactic, and the results are impressive. Adventism remains large, wealthy, and well-branded while simultaneously unable to reach the emerging culture that surrounds it. For all our mechanistic power, we are impotent in reaching the metamodern next door. And of the post-human era fast approaching? I think it goes without saying that if the church lost touch "here," it will have no voice when we get "there."

In short, the local church is broken. The tank has stopped moving.

So then, how are we to contend with this? How can we reach a culture and invite them into the experience of the church if we are so lost ourselves? I propose a solution that begins at reframing what we mean by church and exploring its purpose in three separate levels, which I refer to as the ontology, mechanism, and motion of the church. I will cover the ontology in this present chapter and then dive into the mechanism and motion in the next.

The Ontology of the Church

What is church? This is a question that has given birth to countless books, sermons, and articles. Historically, church has been an institution in either the social establishment tethered to government or as a self-standing entity fettered to its constituents and layered with policies and governance. This has led to a modern reaction toward a more organic, untrammeled expression of church in which "Jesus but not religion" and "church without the hierarchy" are the mantras. However, the ontology of church cannot be unraveled either in its historical makeup nor in its modern reactionary expressions. The ontology of church is essentially other and must be understood as originating in the heart of God.

In this sense, we can only understand the ontology of church if we have grasped the ontology of God. And herein the problem begins. For much of Christianity, God's ontology has been rooted in imperial frameworks that revolve around power, control, and authority. Thus, church comes to be an extension of this supposed axiom. In historic Christianity, the church becomes a means through which empire is controlled. In Protestant Christianity, a similar phenomenon unfolds among the magisterial reformers, for whom church was likewise united to state to enforce its dogmas and act out its coercive ontology of God.

These churches naturally trended toward what Kierkegaard protested as "fashionable tradition" in that everything they were meant to be eventually boiled down to what they had become—mindless rituals, repetitive liturgies, and mission-less entities with rules for membership that did not transcend the external formalities that had been agreed upon. Even today, decades removed from Christendom's state-church, we find that new, untethered expressions of church are facing the same dilemmas.

At the root of all this, I echo that for many, the church is an extension of the imperial God they worship. As a result, the church comes to reflect this God in its activity and priorities. And for most Christians, God has historically been seen as an emperor with a specific set of demands. Whether it is the God of Catholicism, transcendent and distant, cold and cruel, or the God of the early reformers, rooted in Augustinian thought and the bed upon which the Calvinist conception of God—replete with all his dictatorial and coercive qualities—was conceived, most people then and now perceive of God as the great bully who can only be pleased through the right conduct of a people who have committed themselves to meet his demands.

And the result of this subconscious view of God is that regardless of what model of church you employ—be it tethered or untethered, organic, or institutional, house churches or seeker churches—you always end up with the same problem. Your church exists for the pacification of this divine totalitarian, which means your church must uphold a certain image to please his sensibilities. In this context, it doesn't matter what model you use, your church will always be trending toward preservation rather than mission. Thus, it is only a matter of time before the enemy creeps in under the cover of darkness, plants the necessary explosives, and cripples the local church. Years pass, and the church continues on—its services, rituals, and practices intact, but its missional impact is nil. The mobility kill has worked.

In light of this, I contend that there remains good news. A mobility kill is just that—a mobility kill. It is not a kill in the classic sense of the word, which means rather than a resurrection, what the church is merely in need of is restoration. And this repair, I contend, must begin at our conception of God, for regardless of what strategies, methodologies, or policies you put in place, the church will always revert back to incarnating the image of God its members embrace.

Thus, if we wish the ontology of church to move from preservation to mission—from self-protection to self-abandonment—then we must of necessity recapture an image of God that is actively other-centered. Our theology must be rethought, and our false ideas exposed and expelled. Because it is only with a right understanding of who God is and what he is like that we can then cultivate local churches that reflect his heart in all its beauty and charm.

In a sense, the heart of God must be the heart of the church. Without this, the church will always remain vulnerable to Satan's mobility kills. Division is easier to instigate when rules are the center of our religion, for this fuels an environment of judgment and accusation. Fanaticism is always easier to inspire when the letter of the law is the obsession of a people who, like the Pharisees, have read the scriptures but missed Jesus. Detachment is always easier to engender when ideology matters more than people.

But if we center ourselves in the heart of God and allow church to become an extension of that heart, everything changes. No longer is church a program, for the heart of God is not a program. No longer is church an event, for the heart of God is not an event. No longer is church a museum, for the heart of God is not a museum. No longer is church an exclusive club, for the heart of God is neither a club nor exclusive. Rather, the church becomes love incarnate in its community, for the heart of God became love incarnate in Jesus. The church becomes a living community, for the heart of God is both living and community. The church becomes an active healer of its neighborhood, for the heart of God is active in healing the wounds of the world. The church becomes a movement, an everyday experience, a people who walk and talk in love and for love and whose entire mission is love to the end of time.

Thus, church goes from institution to motion, from bureaucracy to relationship, from detached to incarnate. From a group of people who pray, "Teach us, O God, more doctrine," to a community that cries out, collectively and individually, "Teach [us], O God... to breathe deeply in faith."[10]

Is there much more to this conversation? Undoubtedly, yes. I do not mean here to oversimplify the challenge of the modern church. Neither do I mean to reject the institution, which I believe is both necessary and unavoidable. All I mean to say, however, is that if we wish to repair the local church, it begins with reconstructing what we believe of God.

For so long as our church perceives God primarily in terms of strictness, standards, and rules, our local church will always trend toward an exclusive club obsessively focused on defending those twisted ideals. But when we come to see God primarily in terms of love, incarnation, and mission, our local church will then be ready to reflect his heart by enacting its essence among its neighbors. And it is this conceptualization that we need if we are ever to repair and restore the tracks and get the tank back into motion.

With this foundation in place, we can now turn to the

center of volume 2: the synthesis that inverts and upends everything, offering our species more than just another religion, but a portal into the very future we work desperately to construct.

_____

Notes.

1. Theopedia, "Soren Kierkegaard,"
    https://www.theopedia.com/soren-kierkegaard.

2. Ibid.

3. Wikipedia, "Theology of Søren Kierkegaard,"
    https://en.wikipedia.org/wiki/Theology_of_S%C3%B8re
    n_Kierkegaard.

4. Owen C. Thomas, "Kierkegaard's Attack upon 'Christendom' and the Episcopal Church," *Anglican Theological Review*, Vol. 65, No. 3 (1983), p. 5.

5. Ibid.

6. Theopedia, "Soren Kierkegaard,"
    https://www.theopedia.com/soren-kierkegaard.

7. Christianity Today, "Soren Kierkegaard, Christian Existentialist,"
    https://www.christianitytoday.com/history/people/theol
    ogians/soren-kierkegaard.html.

8. Theopedia, "Soren Kierkegaard,"

https://www.theopedia.com/soren-kierkegaard.

9. Ibid.

10. Christianity Today, "Soren Kierkegaard, Christian Existentialist," https://www.christianitytoday.com/history/people/theol ogians/soren-kierkegaard.html.

Chapter 8:

POSTHUMAN

"We must cultivate our garden."
- Voltaire

For decades, denominational leaders have been attempting to unravel the complex reasons why young people leave the church. In recent years, the task of understanding why the church fails to retain millennials or reach the emerging post-church culture has also amplified. And now, new reports indicate that, unlike older generations, millennials who leave church are not coming back when they have children or face other life-altering events.[1] In an attempt to discover a solution to these increasing problems faced by the Western church, however, we have merely found the problem to be overwhelmingly complex, with no one-size-fits-all answer or solution. However, there is a simple, pragmatic paradigm that can give us a necessary platform from which to operate and which I believe can afford us a greater level of success.

Throughout the years, many youth leaders and well-meaning members have assumed that the problem with the church is that it's just too boring, outdated, and irrelevant. Consequently, significant effort has been put into making church fun. It usually involves introducing elements such as a contemporary worship band, sermon series based on popular movies, pastors in the latest fashion who use lots of buzzwords, a more relaxed dress code (or no code whatsoever), and replacing pews with modern seating and sometimes round tables. Now, granted, none of these things are bad in and of themselves. However, the tragedy of this scenario is that after decades of upgrading the church this way, youth are still leaving, and the surrounding culture is still hiding from us. It appears the makeover hasn't worked, which can only mean one thing: something deeper is at play.

And what is this "something deeper"? I will return to this at the close of the chapter. For now, I want to reiterate the key points on the church's ontology and then move on to its mechanism and manifestation.

The ontology, we discovered, is the very character of God. When we see who he is and what he is like, church then becomes an extension of his heart. Sadly, in the modern age, church is treated as an event or program when the truth is, church is much deeper. Others have captured this vision of the church by returning to the Greek word *ecclesia*, which means "group of people," "assembly," or "called-out ones." Such thinkers argue that the church is not a building or event but rather a community. Church, in this sense, is not something we go to but rather something we are. And with this rediscovered vision of the church, we set out to be the church in every facet and moment of life. Church is no longer confined to a weekend service but instead is liberated from those constraints to once again become our identity.

However, the concept of church is deeper still. In fact, it's so deep I can't possibly do it justice in this present book. For that, I have written an entirely different book focused exclusively on the mystery of the church. It's titled "hidden.", and you can learn more about it at the end of this book.

For now, allow me to do my best to anchor us in a deeper vision of the church in the few pages that remain. The return to the Greek *ecclesia* may be a huge step in the right direction, but the journey is far from over, for church, at its very core, is not simply something we are. Instead, church is an extension of who God is. It is a manifestation of his desire to be with us so that, as the church, we enact the very heart of God on the earth. In this sense, the transcendent becomes immanent—the ethereal, real. God is no longer a thing to be philosophized but a being to be experienced in his *ecclesia*, for his *ecclesia* is an extension of himself. Thus, it's not simply that we are church but that the church is God's heart in motion through the brokenness and absurdity of what it means to be human. ·

In this sense, the pattern for how church should function is not to be found in the book of Acts alone but in the life of Jesus, who is God in human flesh, immersed in social action. The way in which Jesus conducted himself while on earth then becomes the very real pattern for how the church ought to conduct itself in its community because the church is the hands and feet of Jesus, which is another way of saying that the church enacts the heart of God in the world. Such a task gives new meaning to Jesus' words, "If you have seen me, you have seen the Father" (John 14:9), as having missional application for us rather than just theological implications for Christ's life. This brings us back to the importance of understanding the heart of God, for in it the church finds its ontological source and purpose.

From that ontology, there then emerges a mechanism and manifestation to which I will now turn.

The Mechanism

Think of a human body. It has a heartbeat that gives it life (yes, it's much more complicated than that, but just go with it for the sake of illustration). However, what if the body had no musculoskeletal system? How would the life that the beating heart gives be of any use? The muscular system of the human body is what enables you to do something with your life. Without it, you would just lay there and have nothing else to do but think all day. With it, you can maneuver yourself through time and space and conduct yourself in a way that impacts the movement of the human story. In other words, the muscular system is like a mechanism that enables you to do something meaningful with the life you have.

The church is much the same. It has an ontology—or heartbeat—in the character of God. This ontology then grounds our purpose and mission, but without a mechanism, the mission will go nowhere. In the Gospels, we see that the mechanism for Jesus accomplishing his mission involves not simply himself but three core friends, another nine disciples, and 70 committed followers. We see that one of the 12 was a treasurer (John 12:6), indicating a level of organization, and that the 12 saw themselves as playing significant roles in the ministry of Jesus. We see the same in the book of Acts, with the church being led by apostles who established churches that were then led by elders and pastors and served by deacons, administrators, and teachers. What we are seeing here from early on are examples of mechanisms—systems that were put in place so that the church could conduct itself in time and space in a way that would reveal the heart of God to its surrounding communities.

In our modern day, the mechanism is global, and so it has a higher level of complexity than the New Testament church. For Adventists, this mechanism involves a General Conference, Divisions, Unions, Local Conferences, Districts, and local churches. Then, within the local church, there is a business meeting, board meeting, and ministry teams. All of this is necessary and part of the mechanism that enables the church to enact its ontology in the world. The mechanism thus emerges from the ontology as a necessary tool to give the ontology practical function and leads us to the final element of the church—its manifestation.

The Manifestation

A human being might have life and strength to enact that life, but when these two come together, there emerges a manifestation of that life. This manifestation involves— among other things—a person's unique expression. The way they style their hair, wear their clothes, their hygiene patterns, and fashion choices—all of these might seem minuscule, but they are also inevitable. As a person enacts their life in the world, they naturally come to reflect the world in which they function, either by rejecting that world, embracing it, or adapting to it. And all of this is reflected in the way in which they manifest themselves.

The church functions the same way. From its ontology and mechanism, the church then manifests itself in its culture or community in a way that reflects its movement in that space. Thus, a church in India will look different from a church in Ohio. A church in the 21st century will look different from a church in the 19th century (or so it should), and so on. In short, the manifestation of the church flows out of its ontology and mechanism acting together in its local setting—whatever that setting might be. It emerges in the way in which the church expresses itself through art, style, and appearance.

Now that I have defined the ontology, mechanism, and manifestation of the church, allow me to return to my initial proposal that something deeper is taking place, preventing youth and post-church culture from connecting with the church. That something deeper is this: somewhere along the way, the church disconnected from its ontological source—the heart of God. As a result, it became more obsessed with preserving than with advancing. The church was no longer a movement but a relic—a museum—with the express purpose of protecting itself and its orthodoxy. As a result, the mechanism of the church went from being the tool through which the heart of God is enacted in the world to the tool through which the church's orthodoxy is preserved and maintained.

Thus, the business meeting went from a missional gathering to move the church forward to a complaint session where members come to whine about the things they don't like. The board meeting took on the same flavor—from missional to preservational—and the ministry teams went from an outward focus to an inward one. As a result of this missing heartbeat and atrophic muscular structure, the church's manifestation moved from communicating the heart of God to the world to maintaining its traditions and customs. Thus, many churches today feel like time capsules from the 1950s. This has not happened in a vacuum but is rather the result of a church with no heartbeat and whose mechanism now exists for its own self-preservation. The end result of these two interactions is a manifestation of irrelevance in the world today.

In the midst of this tragic development, well-meaning members and youth leaders—tired of seeing the young and unchurched increasingly excluded—decided it was time to do something. Unfortunately, rather than return to the ontology of the church and seek to reconstruct a vision of the church from there, many focused exclusively on the church's manifestation. Their aim was to change the church's style, make it more fun and up to date so that the youth would stay. Thus, bands, trendy youth pastors, and round table gatherings became the thing. But decades have passed since these experiments began, and the church is still losing most of its youth. Shifting the manifestation of the church has done little to lower the youth exodus because, once the euphoria of a new and hip church wears off, the youth discern that the church is just as dead as ever—only it has had a makeover to give the appearance of life.

I am not against modern expressions of worship and faith. In fact, I am quite modern myself. I don't like dressing up for church (in fact, I disagree with it), I am not a big fan of pews, liturgy, or all of the behavioral trinkets that come with conservative Adventism. I like contemporary bands, I dress contemporary-casual, and if getting tattoos wouldn't give my mom a heart attack, I would have got some already.

I say this only to emphasize that this is not some anti-contemporary Christian chapter. I am very much in favor of all this. Instead, my objective is deeper—I want to call the church to do more than merely adapt its manifestation. Instead, we need to go back and rediscover our ontology. Because until we do, our churches will either be dead traditional museums or dead traditional museums with a contemporary makeover. Either way, we are still dead. Until the church rediscovers its essence as an extension of God's heart, where each member is called to use their gifts as part of a mechanism that enacts that heart in real time, it will continue to hemorrhage youth, regardless of what clever things we do with its style, art, and appearance.

The Posthuman Longing: A Desire to Transcend Ourselves

In order to bring this point home, we need to return to the posthuman anxiety and allow the doctrine of the church to intersect with the gospel in such a way that it speaks directly to those emerging anxieties—not merely soothing them but inverting them into cosmic meaning and purpose.

Recall from our work so far that the posthumanist

movement is not simply about technology—it is about the human condition. At its core, posthumanism is driven by the same fundamental anxieties that have haunted humanity since the dawn of time. The only difference is that these anxieties are now pressed through the filter of our modern consciousness, nurtured in a post-nuclear, ecologically apocalyptic, cosmically dangerous world. This, in turn, gives rise to the fear of extinction. The way posthumanism contends with this fear is to pursue the act of becoming more than human—to upgrade our biology, to merge with machines—engineering marvels driven by a fear that we are fragile, temporary, and ultimately doomed to disappear.

Closely related is the emerging pursuit of anti-aging technology. This goes further than Botox and anti-wrinkle creams. While the first draft of anti-aging has been predominantly aesthetic, scientists and tech billionaires are now investing billions into "curing aging" itself through gene editing and biological hacking. We are moving from a culture that resists aging to a culture that reverses it. And while there is much to criticize in this, we can't deny its redemptive qualities—that at some level, a post-religious humanity recognizes what scripture has long declared: death is an enemy.

But achieving biological immortality is not enough. We also need to enhance our capacities. Neurologically implanted AI, cybernetics, and genetic enhancements all promise a future where we are stronger, smarter, and no longer bound by our weaknesses. This future is rooted in the transhuman belief that we are not yet finished as a species. There is a next step, a higher version of ourselves waiting to be unlocked. But we can't wait for nature to unlock this for us—we must take control of it ourselves.

All of these desires—immortality, transcendence, self-perfection—are deeply religious impulses masquerading as technological progress. But the question is: What if the very things posthumanists seek have already been answered in Christ?

The answer to that question is the heartbeat of this present volume. And it is the key to birthing a church experience in which the gospel, the alternative community, and the anxieties of posthumanism intersect to offer the world something infinitely better than its corporations and scientists could ever imagine.

Jesus: The Original Posthuman

Here's the main point I want to emphasize. If you forget everything else in this volume, do not forget this. For here lies the *synthesis* that connects the gospel to the anxieties of the next 30 years.

If posthumanism is about transcending humanity's limitations in order to secure ourselves against the pitiless forces of extinction, then Jesus is the prototype—the original posthuman. He is the answer to the anxiety, the anchor against extinction, the way to our highest ideas, the truth that liberates us from our corrupt simulation, and the life that conquers disease, and aging, and death itself.

But instead of blending man with machine, he

accomplished something infinitely better. Christ fused the mortal with the divine. In his humanity, we find the perfect integration of man with God, of that created with the creator.

Allow me to explain this briefly. In Jesus, divinity and humanity merged. He was fully God and fully man, the infinite clothed in the finite, the immortal dwelling within the temporal. What transhumanists long to achieve through artificial evolution, God has already accomplished—not through technology, but through Christ.

And because of this divine-human fusion, Jesus does not simply extend life through biotech—he overcomes death itself. Where posthumanists hope to slow biological aging, Jesus offers the end of death altogether. Not just more years, but a universe cleansed of the virus of death entirely.

What would such a universe look like? What would this mean for interplanetary migration? Terraforming worlds? Expansion as a species? What would this mean for civilization? A cosmos without death, without fear of disease, murder, or war? Life-extensionism might succeed in reversing the natural decay of time, but it is a quasi-immortality at best. We are still vulnerable to viral threats, violence, and accidents. But in Jesus, death itself is gone. The code of reality is rewritten. We cannot even begin to fathom the nuances of such an existence.

But the whole thing is rooted here: Jesus is not simply an upgraded version of *homo sapiens*—he is the firstborn of a new creation (Col. 1:18). His resurrected body is something beyond what we are now—something incorruptible, eternal, and infinite. He remains physical and yet is capable of an inter-dual-dimensional existence, tapping back and forth between this plane and another. The post-resurrection Jesus can therefore be touched and felt. He can eat and drink. But he can likewise enter the upper room despite all the entries being barred and locked. He can veil his appearance. He can vanish and appear in various locations as if he were teleporting.

But none of this is the point. The point is that Jesus created a new humanity in himself—a humanity that had never before existed. Not an upgrade, but a re-engineering altogether. And this humanity, rooted in oneness with the Creator and driven by the impulse of love, he now offers to us. He is the new human. The original posthuman. And he invites his followers to be adopted into his new humanity and, through relationship, to be re-shaped and transformed into the image of the new human.

In other words, posthumanists believe they are pioneering the next step in human evolution, but the real evolutionary leap has already occurred in Christ. He is the second Adam (1 Cor. 15:45), the beginning of a new kind of humanity—not one engineered in laboratories, but reborn through his life, death, and resurrection.

What posthumanism attempts to promise—immortality, transcendence, and human perfection—Jesus has already secured. But unlike the secular vision of the posthuman, Jesus' transformation is not cold, mechanical, or self-deprecating—it is relational, communal, and richly human.

He is our *synthesis*.

The Church: The Failed Manifestation of the True Posthuman Vision

But as amazing as all this is, there is a tragedy to this story. If the church is meant to be the body of Christ, then we are meant to be the manifestation of this new humanity. We should be the community that lives out the reality that Christ accomplished—one no longer bound by the old structures of injustice, power struggles, and the impulse of self.

But we are not.

Instead of an alternative community rooted in the new humanity of Jesus, we mirror the judgmental, power-hungry, interpersonal tensions of the imperial structures we inhabit.

Instead of transcendence—of revealing the divine-human fusion that Jesus embodied—we argue over styles of worship and policy.

Instead of fearlessness in the face of death, we cling to our own institutional survival as if we are just another human empire doomed to extinction.

Instead of a new humanity, we have fallen for the counterfeits: legalism, perfectionism, and the dogmatic venom of Last Generation Theology. The world is looking for transformation, but we have reduced salvation to rules, behaviors, and Eurocentric value structures rather than the radical, supernatural, love-centered re-creation of being that Jesus inaugurated.

In short, we were meant to be the answer to the world's deepest existential anxieties. Instead, we have settled for mediocrity. The world dreams of transcending itself, but the church—rather than proclaiming Christ as the true path of transcendence—has locked itself in an irrelevant, toxic, self-preserving cycle.

And this is why the world turns to AI, genetic engineering, and cybernetic upgrades—because the people who were meant to be the true posthumanists have exchanged their calling for the petty and small.

Reclaiming the Church's True Identity

This is why I must insist: if the church is to regain its relevance, it must do more than update its style—it must rediscover its ontology. It must become the community where the new humanity is visible and tangible:

A people who embody radical love instead of empty religion.

A people whose lives are marked by hope beyond death, not fear of the future.

A people whose mission is restoration, not preservation.

A people who show the world that the longing to transcend can never be fulfilled by machines, but only by

Christ.

We don't need to compete with Silicon Valley for a vision of the future—we need to show the world that the future has already arrived in Jesus.

And until we do, the world will keep looking elsewhere.

I want to close this chapter with the words of the French Enlightenment writer François-Marie Arouet—more commonly known by his stage name, Voltaire—when he wrote at the conclusion of his novel *Candide, ou l'Optimisme* the famous line: "We must cultivate our garden."[2]

Adam Gopnik of *The New Yorker* explains Voltaire's sentiment, saying that what the Frenchman aimed to conceptualize was "that our responsibility is local, and concentrated on immediate action."[3]

When we take into account that much of Voltaire's work was in protest of the established church, which perpetuated suffering and injustice in the name of God, it becomes apparent that, despite his animosity toward Christianity, Voltaire's words can actually guide the modern church toward a recapturing of its intended essence.

The church, as a garden, must not simply be beautified with a new assortment of lilies and roses but must, of necessity, be stripped back to its soil, re-fertilized, and watered—all with the aim of cultivating a garden that contains only the seeds of love, mission, and truth. We must get rid of the weeds of human tradition, the vines of human customs, and the overgrown brush of irrelevant programming. We must cultivate our garden, yes, toward a rediscovery of the heart of God, of which we, the church, are but a mere—albeit immeasurable—extension.

Because it turns out that even in the posthuman age, with all its marvel and complexity, the answer to the longing of the human heart remains the same: *Jesus*.

In him, everything is made new.

———

Notes.

1. Christine Emba, "Why Millennials Are Skipping Church and Not Going Back," The Washington Post.

2. Voltaire, Candide, ou l'Optimisme (Paris: Cramer, 1759).

3. Adam Gopnik, "Voltaire's Garden," The New Yorker.

Vol. 2

Chapter 9:

EXTENSION

---

*"The reason most people don't go to church
is because they've already been."*
- Mark Twain

B efore moving on from the concept and practice of church, there's one more angle we need to explore. This is the broader trajectory of the church today—a shift that extends beyond Adventism but still impacts our movement in significant ways. In this final chapter on the church and absurdity, my goal is to revisit its ontology, mechanism, and manifestation through a wider cultural lens. By doing so, we can better understand the rise of post-church ideology and what philosopher Robert Pasnau calls the age of "after certainty."[1]

As previously explored, the church is an extension of the new humanity of Jesus in time and space—his metaphorical hands and feet. As an expression of his heart, the church must be deeply invested in knowing and embodying that humanity. Without a true understanding of it, the church cannot reflect its beauty in the world. A distorted view of God inevitably shapes church governance and practice in ways that mirror the false rather than the true. Knowing the heart of God, then, is not just a theological exercise but a lived reality—one that must be experienced in and among the world.

The more the church aligns with the heart of God, the more it can conduct itself in harmony with that heart. The church becomes a reflection of what it beholds, whether good or evil. The mechanism of the church emerges as the pragmatic methodology by which it directs itself in its sphere of influence toward the goal of being the heart of God in that space. This, in turn, shapes how the church is manifested in its neighborhood, community, and culture.

Practically speaking, if a church is to develop a meaningful mechanism and manifest itself in a redemptive way, it must first revisit its ontology. We cannot begin the conversation at manifestation—as so many have—only to get caught in endless debates over style, traditions, and worship practices. These debates fuel division, stall mission, and ultimately lead to stagnation. The cycle repeats itself with books, seminars, sermons, articles, and YouTube uploads, all dissecting surface-level issues while the deeper crisis remains unaddressed—the expected end of what Constantine once referred to as "the fruit of a misused leisure."[2]

But once the ontology is revisited and the church seeks to pattern its movement and action after the heart of God—truly becoming an extension of him in the world—it will naturally become what Jesus became. To explain the significance of this in the context of secular outreach, I must first establish the foundation for what I have already referred to as the contemporary overarching motion of the church.

The Contemporary Overarching Motion of the Church

It is neither surprising nor controversial to suggest that the contemporary overarching motion of the church–at least in the West–is increasingly split in two polarizing directions. These directions are so antithetical to one another that, for the first time in my life, I am beginning to see the words of Jesus come closer to realization: that in the last days, "many will turn away from the faith and will betray and hate each other" (Matt. 24:10). The polarization I am referring to is none other than the unification of the church with human empire.

While this is a topic on which many sincere and honest Christians differ–and one that is filled with complexities and nuances–I want to paint a broad picture that captures how many secular Western minds perceive the current tensions between church and government. That picture is this: the church is reaching for political power, seeking to legislate its moral framework and impose it on society through coercion. In Adventist terms, evangelical Protestantism is extending its arms toward metaphorical– and eventually literal–Rome.

It is in light of this present reality that popular evangelical influencer Beth Moore could say that "evangelicalism has, broadly speaking, 'colossally blown it.'"[3] By "it," Moore is referring to the church's mission and witness, which she surmises is in "humiliating need of reform."[4] This same sentiment is shared by pastor Matt Chandler, who, in his *Vice* interview titled "What Is the Future of Evangelicalism?" bluntly stated:

You're going to see what we've already seen probably three or four times in Christian history. There are going to be those that try and reach the world by becoming like the world, and then there are going to be those that try to, by the grace of God, hold fast to orthodox Christian faith in a way that's compassionate and kind, and they're going to have to weather the backlash of all the wrong that's been done in the name of Jesus the last 50 years.[5]

In short, Chandler has just introduced two evangelicalisms in the contemporary age—one that compromises with the world (by which Chandler is referring to politics, coercion, and power struggles) and one that tries to be like Jesus. As we move further along in history, the true church will not only be in conflict with the false but will also find itself in conflict with a secular world that accuses it of the same wrongs committed by its apostate counterpart.

Adventism as a movement has long held to a similar view, known as *remnant theology*, in which the final struggle is depicted as a conflict between true and false Christianity. Ellen White expressed this concept best in *The Great Controversy* when, speaking of the latter days, she revealed that "apostate Protestantism" would emerge "when the Protestant churches shall seek the aid of the civil power for the enforcement of their dogmas."[6] Elsewhere, White states that "when Protestant churches shall seek the support of the secular power" for the purpose of what the White Estate refers to as the "enforce[ment of] oppressive measures,"[7] there "will be a national apostasy which will end only in national ruin."[8]

In short, Adventism's end-time vision is that "apostate Protestantism" in the contemporary age "will pursue a similar course"[9] to that of the ancient Roman church. Thus, in harmony with Chandler's analysis, White states that "all Christendom will be divided into two great classes."[10] This division will present to the world a church thirsty for legislative authority—hypocritical, judgmental, and rooted in a coercive ontology. The tragic result of such a course, White reveals, is that the church itself shall "become the sport of infidels and skeptics because so many who bear its name are ignorant of its principles."[11]

And it is this sad reality that marks the contemporary overarching narrative of the church as seen through the eyes of the unchurched. Regardless of the authenticity of faith and the narrative of scripture, what most see is a church in which "Carries Trump to Historic Victory"[12] with the goal of amassing state power to themselves as they combat what they perceive as the threat of "liberalism." This act has been likened to Esau selling his birthright for a pot of stew, in that the modern church has sold its values, morals, and soul for access to the Oval Office.

The most compelling part of the whole debacle is that, despite the ways in which the church has undergone a makeover to brand itself as modern by adapting its manifestation to the cultural milieu, the culture now sees through the mask and finds that, beneath the external manifestation of the church, there nevertheless lies a distasteful ontology. Thus, former evangelical Levi Rogers could state:

While on the surface, many of these churches sport

tattoos, rock music, and a trendy hipster exterior, underneath this flashy veneer often lies the same foundation of conservative fundamentalism.[13]

Rogers goes on to state that "when the ideals of brotherly love, grace, and mercy are traded in for the gods of power, theological dogma, and nationalism, I feel like I can no longer recognize the faith I grew up with."[14]

In her article titled "11 Former Evangelicals Talk About What They Left Behind," author Dani Fankhauser quotes former evangelicals on the reasons they left the church. One theme to emerge is what one interviewee refers to as the teachings of Jesus being "in diametrical opposition to the popular teachings of the well-known evangelical celebrities of today"[15]–teachings that Paul Prather referred to as "stances [that] repel millions."[16] Prather goes on to state:

> [Y]es, young people are leaving the pews in droves because too often the person facing them in those pews is a fraud ... anytime you replace the spectacularly good news of God's love, grace, and mercy with fury, condemnation, and political gamesmanship, you turn people away from the very kingdom of heaven you think you're promoting.[17]

During Trump's first term, the drama intensified when *Christianity Today*–the magazine founded by legendary evangelist Billy Graham–responded to Trump's impeachment by calling for his removal from office. Mark Galli, author of the editorial, summarized his position well when he wrote that "Christians have a responsibility to call out Trump's immoral behavior. Otherwise, they risk damaging their ability to share the Gospel with the world."[18]

However, to an onlooking generation, the damage has already been done. What were once scattered anecdotes of judgmentalism and hypocrisy in the church have become a full-scale display—an open exhibition of a movement that was meant to usher in not the rise of human empire, but its ultimate undoing through the arrival of a kingdom fundamentally at odds with the principles of human governance. A kingdom so radically *other* that neither the left nor the right could ever fully align with it.

But this kingdom is not being proclaimed. Instead, the contemporary motion of the church is consumed by a political power grab, driven by false theological constructs that distort its very foundation. The God it professes to follow has been reshaped into an image more concerned with authority than mercy, more defined by power than servanthood, and more preoccupied with judgment than love—all in the name of national and imperial stability.

So how does Adventism fit into this milieu? I believe that our movement is a prophetic movement, and as such, we have a responsibility to prophesy against the unification of Jerusalem with Athens—of the kingdom of God with the empire of man. As a church that was born, bred, and birthed with the mission of understanding the heart of God, we are therefore in a position to enact his heart in the world in a way no other church is doing—particularly as other churches align themselves with partisan agendas, excluding and demonizing those who oppose them. And before conservative readers throw this book in the bin for pushing liberal propaganda, let me be clear: the position I espouse applies as much to the left as to the right.

In summary, it appears the contemporary motion of the church has brought new meaning to Mark Twain's adage, "The reason most people don't go to church is because they've already been."

Twain—a sharp critic of organized religion—was no stranger to its hypocrisy. In his mind, those who had attended church had already found all the reasons necessary to leave.

In the modern age, I would say that the reason most people don't go to church is because the church has already come to them—and it was angry. If ever there was a time to reveal the heart of God to the world, if ever the final manifestation of his character needed to be on display, it is now.

_____

Notes.

1. Brice Ezell, "Is There Hope for Knowledge? On Robert Pasnau's After Certainty," The New Republic.

2. Roland Herbert Bainton, Christianity (New York: Houghton Mifflin), 95.

3. "Beth Moore: 'Evangelicalism Is in Humiliating Need of

Reform'," Relevant Magazine.

4. Ibid.

5. Vice, "What Is the Future of Evangelicalism?"

6. Ellen G. White, The Great Controversy (Mountain View, CA: Pacific Press Publishing Association), 445.

7. Ellen G. White, Testimonies for the Church, Vol. 5 (Mountain View, CA: Pacific Press Publishing Association), 7.

8. Ellen G. White, The Spirit of Prophecy, Vol. 4 (Battle Creek, MI: Seventh-day Adventist Publishing Association), 410.

9. Ellen G. White, The Great Controversy, 615.

10. Ibid., 450.

11. Ibid., 463.

12. "Decisive Christian Vote Carries Trump to Historic Victory, Post-Election Research Shows," Arizona Christian University.

13. Levi Rogers, "Why I'm Leaving the Evangelical Church."

14. Ibid.

Vol. 2

15. Dani Fankhauser, "11 Former Evangelicals Talk About What They Left Behind."

16. Paul Prather, "Thanks to Politics, Churches Have Run Off Their Young Adults–And Potential Converts, Too."

17. Ibid.

18. Emma Green, "How Trump Lost an Evangelical Stalwart," The Atlantic.

Chapter 10:

TRAPPED

"A man may die, nations may rise and fall, but an idea lives on. Ideas have endurance without death."
– John F. Kennedy

In the previous chapter, we transitioned from the concept of the church to the concept of the remnant. In doing so, I assumed a general acceptance of remnant theology. But the truth is, this doctrine is one of the least popular within Adventism itself, with most millennial Adventists finding it distasteful.[1] It has also fueled evangelical hostility toward Adventism, making meaningful connection with them more difficult.

At the same time, remnant theology–the belief that the Seventh-day Adventist Church is the only true church at the end of time and a prophetic movement predicted in Revelation–has fostered a sectarian, narcissistic attitude in previous generations. This mindset is now being increasingly rejected by younger Adventists. In a postmodern society, where truth is seen as subjective and exclusivity is often equated with arrogance, the idea of a remnant church carries assumptions that many find repulsive.

Few examples highlight the divisiveness of sectarian ideology more than the ongoing conflict between Christianity, Judaism, and Islam—three major traditions, each claiming to possess ultimate truth. The hostility, indifference, and violence that have often emerged from these religious claims have led many in secular culture to embrace Nietzsche's perspective: that religion fosters division rather than unity, and that where reason could promote peace, faith instead fuels conflict. It's no surprise, then, that Nietzsche is often considered a forerunner of postmodernism, his critique of absolute truth shaping much of contemporary thought. While many religious individuals reject this conclusion outright, a closer look reveals an underlying cultural longing for harmony—one that religion has often undermined.

For Nietzsche, as well as for many secular and postmodern thinkers, the very assertion of absolute truth is the seedbed of injustice and oppression. This means that in our interactions with the secular world—whether through evangelism or Bible study—the notion of a remnant church claiming to have exclusive truth sets off immediate red flags. To many, it signals militancy, separatism, and supremacy—qualities that often drive seekers away before they even hear the message.

Despite these tensions, some insist on holding to this doctrine in its traditional form. But doing so often comes at the cost of relationships. In reaction to this rigid stance, many in emerging generations have swung to the opposite extreme—rejecting remnant theology altogether. Yet in doing so, they risk losing something valuable (which we will explore in the next chapter).

The goal of this chapter, then, is to revisit remnant theology and offer a reframing that makes it both compelling and meaningful for Adventist millennials and secular seekers alike. To do this, we will establish three key foundations:

1. The Permanence and Essence Of Ideas

2. The Necessary Coherence of Ideas

3. The Somatic Embodiment of Ideas

These three concepts will help us reshape remnant theology into something that speaks to the modern world without sacrificing its core truth.

The Permanence and Essence of Ideas

Civil Rights activist Medgar Evers once said, "You can kill a man, but you can't kill an idea."[2] This truth is so self-evident it barely requires defense. But if, against the obvious axioms of life, you doubt its validity, history is always there to prove you wrong. Time and again, violence, oppression, and coercion have failed to stamp out the advance of ideas.

The birth of Christianity is a perfect example. As Tertullian famously observed of the persecuted and emaciated church, "The blood of martyrs is… seed."[3] The more Rome tried to silence the gospel, the faster it spread. But this isn't unique to Christianity. Countless religious movements have endured brutal persecution, only to expand. The war on terror has been dubbed an ideological war because the true enemy is not an army–it's an idea. Military force has done little to slow its spread, just as the fall of the Third Reich did not erase Aryanism, nor did the defeat of Jim Crow end racism. In fact, white supremacy is on the rise in the very nation that led Hitler's defeat and later declared segregation unconstitutional. And if these examples aren't enough, consider this: despite overwhelming scientific and social ridicule, there is still–somehow–a Flat Earth Society.

There seems to be a universal axiom at play: *ideas do not die*. But it's not just their resilience that makes them immortal–it's their very nature. Ideas cannot be contained by physical barriers. There is no wall, no fortress, no prison cell that can restrain them. They move freely, passing through borders and defenses, seeking hosts who will embrace them. Ideas–like disembodied specters–drift effortlessly through our manufactured barricades, expanding their reach in ways that brute force cannot stop.

This is precisely why Malala Yousafzai has argued that Islamic extremism cannot be defeated through violence, only through education. The incorporeal can only be dismantled by what is equally intangible–an opposing idea. In short, ideas transcend physics. They cannot be physically restrained, and they certainly cannot be repelled through force alone.

Understanding this foundational truth–that ideas never die and cannot be contained–allows us to enter into the next concept.

The Necessary Coherence of Ideas

Back in 2008, one of the most popular television series was Lost. The show followed a group of plane crash survivors stranded on a mysterious island filled with secrets and unexplained phenomena, keeping viewers on the edge of their seats. But when the series finale aired, it sparked widespread anger and frustration. The plotlines had become so tangled that the writers seemed unable to resolve them in a satisfying way. The story's coherence unraveled to such a degree that, as the credits rolled, viewers were left with a mountain of unanswered questions and unresolved plot holes.[4] The backlash was so intense that one of the show's writers eventually deleted his Twitter account due to the flood of hate messages.[5]

This reaction highlights a simple truth: as human beings, we don't just love stories—we crave stories that make sense. When we invest in a narrative, we expect a rhythm, a flow, a sense of internal logic that carries us forward. Stories riddled with contradictions and plot holes frustrate us. Coherent stories, on the other hand, become classics— memorable tales passed down through generations.

But this need for coherence doesn't just apply to storytelling. Ideas, too, need cohesion. Without internal consistency, an idea loses its power. If a worldview is contradictory or fragmented, it collapses under scrutiny. For any belief system to be taken seriously, it must hold together.

Few have captured the importance of coherence as

effectively as the founders of TED Talks. TED is not just a stage for speakers—it follows a strict model designed for clarity and impact. In TED Talks: The Official TED Guide to Public Speaking, organizers emphasize that every talk must communicate one key idea and nothing more. This forces speakers to focus, ensuring that each 15-minute talk is a cohesive narrative, reinforced by research, anecdotes, and illustrations that all tie back to the main point. The result? TED Talks have become a global source of compelling content, demonstrating that structured clarity is the key to making an idea resonate.

Despite the rise of postmodernism—with its fluid approach to truth and skepticism toward meta-narratives—most people still instinctively seek coherence. They long for a framework that helps them make sense of the chaos and absurdity of life. This need for consistency, both in stories and in worldviews, is why remnant theology is not just a compelling idea—it's an incredibly meaningful one.

The Somatic Embodiment of Ideas

Ideas are imperishable, non-corporeal, and necessarily rhythmic—but there is one more crucial aspect that cannot be ignored: they require a host. Once embodied, ideas take shape in tangible, practical ways. While they may begin as abstract concepts, they do not remain that way. Instead, they become real through the conduct of those who live them out. An idea moves from the theoretical to the actual the moment it finds a somatic manifestation—a person who embodies and enacts it in their sphere of influence.

No idea worth its salt remains purely abstract. Ideas that do not take root in action tend to fade into obscurity, lingering only in academic circles. But for an idea to have real cultural impact, it must move from the abstract to the sensory, from the theoretical to the experiential. It must become something that both a philosopher and a stay-at-home parent—with bills to pay and kids to raise—can find meaning in. Ultimately, regardless of how compelling an idea may sound in theory, it is judged by its practical outcomes.

This is why communism, despite its utopian promise, has been rejected by so many. Theoretically, it presents an appealing vision of justice and equality. But in practice, it has never manifested anything close to utopia.[6] The same critique applies to Christianity. While the teachings of Jesus are undeniably beautiful, much of Christendom has failed to embody them in a way that makes the faith desirable or compelling. (But I'm getting ahead of myself.)

In short, the somatic embodiment of ideas is the process by which abstract concepts are lived out in the chaos of life. Over time, as more people embody an idea, patterns emerge—patterns that determine whether the idea produces flourishing or harm. And eventually, most people judge an idea not by its theoretical promise, but by its lived reality.

Now that we have explored these three foundations—the permanence of ideas, the necessity of coherence, and their embodiment in action—we must ask: how do these shape our understanding of remnant theology? In the next chapter, we will see how these principles—each self-evident—naturally lead to a theological construct that is both meaningful and necessary. But before we move forward, allow me to briefly demonstrate how they reframe the doctrine of the remnant itself.

John F. Kennedy once said:

> A man may die, nations may rise and fall, but an idea lives on. Ideas have endurance without death.[7]

Captured within this statement is the permanence and transcendence of ideas—concepts we have already explored. Ideas do not perish with the fall of institutions, movements, or even civilizations. They outlive them.

This means that if there is to be a remnant church at the end of time, its meaning cannot be confined to a physical institution. It must transcend organizational structures and exist as a dynamic, living reality.

This challenges the common assumption that the remnant is synonymous with the Adventist institution. It is not. The remnant is an idea in motion—a reality that cannot be contained, restrained, or trademarked. Shifting our perspective in this way allows us to reimagine remnant theology in a way that avoids the sectarian and self-congratulatory pitfalls that have plagued its historical development. It invites us to experience the remnant as something that glorifies God rather than ourselves—as a way of being that transforms the world rather than isolates from it.

The fundamental problem with how remnant theology is often presented is that it has been institutionalized—trapped within the borders of Adventism as a brand identity. This approach distorts the very story the doctrine is meant to tell. Worse, it often results in a practical application that perpetuates injustice rather than confronting it.

In the next chapter, we will explore these implications further—and uncover a way forward.

———

Notes.

1. Barna Group. Adventist Millennial Study, p. 42.

2. Robert Koehler. "You Can't Kill an Idea." Chicago Tribune.

3. Tertullian. Apologeticus, ch. 50.

4. Jarred Keller. "Fans Split on Masterful, Frustrating 'Lost' Finale." Pacific Standard.

5. Andrew Sims. "Damon Lindelof Exits Twitter—Possibly Due to Continued Outcry Over 'LOST' Finale." Hypable.

6. Ilya Somin. "Lessons from a Century of Communism." The Washington Post.

7. "You Cannot Kill an Idea." TV Tropes.

Chapter 11:

STORY

"The value of an idea lies in the using of it."
– Thomas Edison

In the previous chapter, I introduced three concepts that have helped me reformulate my approach to remnant theology—one that avoids both the historic sectarian approach and the modern reactionary trend of "just get rid of the whole thing." I referred to these three ideas as:

1. The Permanence and Essence of Ideas

2. The Necessary Coherence of Ideas

3. The Somatic Embodiment of Ideas

The first concept is simple: ideas are inherently non-corporeal and, as a result, cannot be contained or bound by physical barriers. Time does not drain them of their force. The second concept speaks to the need for ideas to function holistically as a narrative, with the pieces fitting together in such a way that a person does not have to endure cognitive dissonance to embrace them. The third emphasizes another obvious assumption—that ideas worth their existence never linger in the abstract but always find a host through which they are materialized in action, patterns, and practice. Any idea that fails to transition from the academic to the practical becomes a mere mental exercise for intellectual sophisticates and holds little meaning or applicability in the urgent realities of life.

But the question I want to answer in this present chapter is: How do these concepts help me reimagine remnant theology? And can they be molded to work in settings where the sectarian version of remnant theology is seen as appalling, narcissistic, and toxic?

As I've mentioned previously in this series, secular culture is so fragmented that there's no way for me to know whether or not the approach I outline here will work in your setting. This is simply how it has worked in mine. However, because the only alternative tends to be the historic approach, I would argue that even if this method doesn't translate perfectly to your context, it will still find a more meaningful reception than the alternative. As always, it's up to the reader to adapt and refine for their immediate circumstances.

Before I share my reimagined approach, keep in mind that the three concepts from the previous chapter (and summarized above) are not ideas I necessarily share with a seeker. They form a conceptual foundation for me, but I don't sit with a secular sojourner and explain these elements before introducing remnant theology. Instead, they quietly undergird my approach, surfacing naturally as I explore the topic. This will become evident as you work through the explanation below.

Reframing Remnant Theology

The way I engage with remnant theology begins with a simple but fundamental principle of historical theology–one that requires no theological expertise or philosophical background to grasp:

Every denomination and religion tells a story.

Once we agree on that premise, I add another layer:

Every denomination and religion tells a different story.

This concept requires a bit more explanation. While some faith traditions share overlapping elements, they exist as distinct movements because enough people resonated with one story over another. Over time, these stories shaped communities, each emphasizing their own unique plotline. Given the diversity of human temperament, experience, and perspective, it's no surprise that history has produced countless religious narratives–some compatible, others in direct contradiction.

At this point, if additional clarification is needed, I introduce the Calvinist/Arminian divide as an example. Instead of using theological jargon, I frame it like this:

- Story A: *God is Power.*

- Story B: *God is Love.*

I demonstrate how these two narratives develop into

completely different pictures of God. I am careful not to attack or criticize opposing views—that's not the goal. If you turn this into a polemic, you will lose most modern secular thinkers. Instead, my objective is to establish a simple reality: different communities of faith tell different faith stories. That's it.

Once that foundation is laid, I ask the next question:

What is the battle between good and evil about?

By this point, we have already explored the Great Controversy in depth, and the seeker understands that the war between good and evil is fundamentally an ideological struggle—truth about God versus lies about God.

So where do these lies exist?

Are they found in paganism? Catholicism? If I wanted to encounter distortions about God, where should I look? The answer is: everywhere.

Lies about God exist in every religious tradition, including Christianity. They are not confined to the Vatican, ancient mythologies, or "infidel" libraries. Ideas transcend boundaries, embedding themselves in religious platitudes and presuppositions across all traditions—including our own.

This concept rarely generates pushback. In fact, many people find it refreshing to hear a Christian admit that he doesn't know everything and that his understanding could be flawed. But from here, I take them to the next question:

If ideas are meant to be coherent, and faith stories should align with the truth, what do we do with the contradictions between "God is Power" and "God is Love"?

One of these stories, by virtue of coherence, cannot be true. While neither may be perfect, it is evident that one of them is significantly influenced by falsehoods about God. When we measure these narratives against everything we have already seen about God's character, it becomes clear that one story perpetuates distortions while the other seeks to uncover the truth.

At this point, things can get uncomfortable, so I shift gears.

Why does any of this matter?

As we explore, my goal is to connect theology to justice and ethics. Our God-story matters because ideas do not remain abstract—they materialize in the real world.

For example:

- If you believe God is a dictator who refuses to be questioned, how will that influence your parenting?

- If you believe God favors one nation over another, does that not lead to nationalism, discrimination, or indifference toward suffering?

- If you believe God is hierarchical and authoritative,

does that not contribute to abusive relationships, patriarchal control, and gender oppression?

- If you believe God is aligned with political conservatism, does that not lead to the dehumanization of alternative parties?

These questions illustrate how theology influences human behavior. Ideas, when embodied, shape actions—and actions shaped by falsehoods about God inevitably lead to injustice.

At this point, I take the seeker back to the competing God-stories in the world. If theology is riddled with colonial constructs and Christ himself has been appropriated as the glue of empire resulting in church-sanctioned injustice, will God not see to it that a new story be told? One that recaptures his heart and dispels the lies that have overshadowed it?

The Remnant as a Story, Not an Institution

This leads to the final point: Remnant theology is not about an institution because ideas cannot be contained within institutions.

The remnant is not a logo, a brand, or a tax ID. It is not owned by a denomination. Instead, it is a story—one that moves into culture, liberating as it flows, unhindered by bureaucratic constraints.

Remnant, therefore, is protest. It is deconstruction. It is

decolonization. It is re-articulation. Rediscovery. Reconstruction. It is a return to the way of the indigenous Jesus who was assassinated by a coalition of left and right allied with the occupying power of the Roman state.

I am not remnant because I belong to a particular denomination. I am remnant because I belong to a healing story that refuses to imperialize Jesus, resists the commodification of messiah, the commercializing of spirituality, and the appropriation of the church as an arm of the state.

This does not mean the institution of Adventism is pointless. Institutions are the somatic embodiment of ideas. As the story spreads, it naturally gathers people who organize themselves into a system to facilitate the telling of the story on a global scale. This leads to hospitals, schools, publishing houses, churches, and ministries—all in service of advancing the story. And this has its place.

But the institution is not the story.

The remnant transcends logos, tax numbers, and denominational structures. It is, first and foremost, an idea— one that rises above all physical boundaries.

With this perspective as the foundation for remnant theology, I have found a way to reject both sectarianism and pluralism, opting instead for a middle approach that is both theologically sound and effective in secular outreach.

The end result, at least for me, is a remnant theology that

rejects theological pluralism, speaks truth to power with boldness, stands in radical solidarity with the oppressed while simultaneously energizing our communities with an anti-sectarian humility that nurtures a unity that is both authentic and liberating for all.

It is toward unity that we now turn.

Chapter 12:

HOMOGENEITY

"Society is not homogenous, and those who do not deliberately close their eyes have to recognise that men differ greatly from one another from the physical, moral, and intellectual viewpoints."
- Vilfredo Pareto

The doctrine of unity is not one that we often turn to when thinking about secular outreach. In the realm of modernist skepticism, Christian apologists turn to natural theology and other philosophical arguments to make a case for the existence of God. It is thought, in this discipline, that if the culture is given enough grounds to see God as the best possible explanation for life and existence, then perhaps this will make said culture easier to reach. I certainly don't doubt the impact and validity of contemporary apologetics, but to suggest that logical or rational argumentation suffices to lead a wandering soul to Christ is certainly an overstatement.

Likewise, in the realm of post- and meta-modernity, cultural apostles invest time in reframing the gospel to speak meaningfully to the secular mind. We invest energy in coming close, listening, understanding, and then contextualizing our approach. In fact, this model is essentially what this entire four-volume set is built on. However, to think that reframing the gospel to interact meaningfully with contemporary sensibilities and value structures suffices to bring the post-church heart to Christ is another example of overconfidence in ideological discourse.

Now, of course, these elements are necessary. There is nothing worse for a secular mind than to contend with a Christian who lacks the capacity to understand her language and speak meaningfully to her heart. Nevertheless, as is the case with rational argumentation, ideological contextualization is simply not enough. Instead, what the culture most desperately needs is a demonstration of divine love in action. It is the pragmatic conduct of the collective Christian mind that provides the greatest evidence and the most effective invitation to the secular seeker. This, I believe, is precisely why—despite all the enlightening ideas revealed in scripture—Jesus laid the evidence of his authenticity as Messiah on the least expected thing when he said: *"By this all men will know that you are My disciples, if you love one another."* (John 13:35)

Adventists quote this verse often, but I'm not so sure we understand it. Jesus is stating that all men will know we are his, not by our prophetic insights, systematic cohesion, evangelistic methodologies, or theological propositions, but by our willingness to bring food to each other when we are sick, pray for each other when we are lonely, embrace each other when facing difficulty, and inconvenience ourselves with no reward to ourselves. Somehow, the tiny and often imperceptible actions of life—the random acts of kindness, the acceptance and listening ear, the caring and providing for one another—are the ones to emerge as the primary evidence of Christ's messianic legitimacy, not the apocalyptic visions of Daniel or Revelation.

However, as is the case with all biblical teachings, the doctrine of unity has been perverted to the point that, rather than attracting the culture, we end up repelling them. Therefore, in my experience connecting with and reaching out to secular minds, I have found it necessary to revisit the topic of unity and discover precisely how God intends for this practical mode of being—at the front and center of the church's universal attractiveness—to function. In doing so, I have uncovered three simple keys that have helped me navigate my own concept of unity from what it has become to what God originally intended it to be. Those three keys I refer to as:

1. The Fallacy of Homogeneity

2. The Paradox of Attachment

3. The Divine Oneness Reflected

In this present chapter, I will comment on the first and expand on the other two in the next.

The Fallacy of Homogeneity

When I was a soldier, one of the values stressed most often for military precision was the value of being "uniform." Uniform, in military culture, refers to much more than the camouflage outfit everyone wears. Rather, in that context, it refers to a culture of single-mindedness and functional predictability. Everything had to be uniform. Our combat gear, barracks, hairstyles, motor pools, and equipment inventories were identical. In combat scenarios, items were stored in the exact same place each time to maximize reaction time during high-stress situations. The entire military structure was set up this way to engineer a culture in which every mind thought and conducted itself the same. This approach increased compliance with the rule of law while decreasing individuality and insubordination—modes of being that had the potential to derail a company from its intended mission.

As far as military operations go, this method works quite well. The military is not something you join for the sake of friendships, emotional and spiritual healing, or to celebrate the uniqueness and diversity of each individual. Instead, the military is a machine with one purpose—to wage war as effectively and efficiently as possible. To that end, emptying each mind of its unique attributes to maximize the reliability of national defense measures was imperative.

However, as brilliant as this approach may be in a military context, it is tragic in just about every other environment. If a parent attempts to raise their children in this manner by repressing their individuality, the results will be disastrous. If home life is to be warm, welcoming, and inviting, individuality must be celebrated and embraced. If a child is to grow with any level of emotional balance and autonomy, their individuality must be nurtured. Likewise, if the church is to succeed in its mission of spreading the gospel, it must come to terms with the celebration of the other—nurturing and empowering the authentic self of each member. In doing so, the gospel moves from a mere ideological construct to a promise revealed in the diversity of life and being.

The tragedy I observe, however, is the disturbing tendency in the church to aim for a militarized environment of uniformity while claiming it is unity. Nothing could be further from the truth.

Author and speaker Ty Gibson said it best when he wrote:

> The unspoken quest to produce the homogenous Christian person—all of us thinking, feeling, vibing, dressing, singing, articulating, expressing within the same narrow cultural spectrum—has the effect of shutting people down and crippling the church's witness.

In this 2020 tweet, Gibson provides an excellent definition and diagnosis of the problem of pursuing uniformity (which he terms homogeneity). This unspoken quest, then, is really a perversion of true unity that masquerades as its ally. Throughout Adventism, this fallacy plagues us, distorting our vision at every step because it takes the biblical concept of unity and morphs it into the authoritarian concept of uniformity.

Unity sees the people of God loving one another, supporting one another, and working together despite their diversity in culture, temperaments, and convictions. The quest for homogeneity, however, insists that we must all be identical. Therefore, all Adventists must sing hymns, and if you don't, you are not a true Adventist. All Adventists must dress like Europeans, and if you don't, you are not a true Adventist. All Adventists must comply with my version of modesty, and if you do not, then you are not a true Adventist—not an authentic one, anyway.

Calling this perversion out is tricky because it is like a slithery snake that quickly hides behind pious phrases like, "Can two walk together except they be agreed?" or "To the law and to the testimony"—a verse often quoted not to defend what is written *according to this word* but to defend what is written *according to my opinion*.

The problem is compounded when we realize that much of what is accepted as traditional Adventist culture is merely a recapitulation of old Euro-American trends. None of our dress, music, or language came to us from heaven. On the contrary, all of it reflects the Anglo North American culture in which Adventism evolved. When we attempt to manufacture a homogenous Adventist culture that reflects this one-dimensional expression—of old suburban men in suits and women in flowery swing dresses—we end up communicating that the only way to be a faithful, godly Adventist is to first dress, sing, and talk like a white person from the 1950s. And anyone who cannot fit into that narrow, oppressive mold is relegated to the pile of worldly, carnal people who reject God's end-time standards.

It is this quest for homogeneity that has ruined our ability, as a church, to be truly united. The moment the youth want to sing Hillsong or the pastor wants to hang up the suit and dress more casually, we go to war in the name of "we must be united" without realizing that unity is not about everyone having the same convictions and expressions. It is about everyone being driven by such a deep love that they can serve, honor, and support one another in the midst of diversity—not its absence.

The fallacy of homogeneity is that it is not true unity because homogeneity removes the necessary elements for unity to thrive. It gets rid of uniqueness, individuality, and diversity, creating a pseudo-unity—one in which the church flows in harmony only so long as no one challenges the pre-approved status quo. And because this status quo often favors a bygone generation, emerging secular and unchurched neighbors who visit our churches find that, despite the potentially insightful message we carry, they simply don't fit in.

This war between unity and uniformity also rages over the theme of women's ordination. Some parts of the world are not culturally prepared to embrace such a progressive step, while others are long overdue for the shift. In an attempt to allow regions to move forward without imposing a value structure on others, the church was asked to vote on a simple proposition: that unions would have the capacity to ordain women to ministry in the regions where they saw fit. But in the lead-up and aftermath of the vote, quasi-unity was evoked as a manipulation tactic to coerce the conscience in the name of homogeneity. The vote, as we know, did not go in favor of women's ordination.

The tables have now turned. The Westerners who once spread their homogeneity onto non-Western cultures by imposing their value structures and perceptions of holiness are now the ones facing the same treatment. Those they once dominated are now the dominant members of the church, returning the favor by imposing their homogeneity onto us. It's a tragic scenario, but the worst part is the myth so many have bought into—that diverse regions operating in diverse ways somehow damage our unity. Nothing could be further from the truth. It is in the absence of diversity that unity is damaged. It is in its presence that unity thrives.

The Italian economist Vilfredo Pareto said it best:

> Society is not homogeneous, and those who do not deliberately close their eyes have to recognize that men differ greatly from one another from the physical, moral, and intellectual viewpoints.[1]

The culture, of course, is fully aware of this diversity. The church, not so much. And this, I believe, is one of the reasons we struggle to connect meaningfully with a post-church age. We are either divided or uniform, and in our quest for uniformity, we only deepen the divide. The world sees this. Division does not attract the skeptic to the cross. Homogeneity does not either—especially when the culture we are contending with values autonomy and self-determination as inviolable human rights. In this context, all displays of homogeneity in the name of unity only serve to fool us. They do not fool the seeker.

To this, some would disagree, suggesting that problems with unity cannot be the cause of our missional failure because unity is not among the chief intellectual concepts in the theological fields people are contending with. But I would remind us of the words of Jesus, who stated that our love for one another is the greatest evidence of his truth. Without this love–which we will explore in more detail in the next chapter–we simply cannot fulfill our mission.

Ellen White expressed this sentiment when she wrote:

> We seldom find two persons exactly alike. Among human beings as well as among the things of the natural world, there is diversity. Unity in diversity among God's children–the manifestation of love and forbearance in spite of difference of disposition–this is the testimony that God sent His Son into the world to save sinners.[2]

It is this ability to love and cherish one another in our diversity that testifies of Jesus' salvific story. This is far from the fallacy of homogeneity. This is, by contrast, a harmonious way of being in which opposites are brought together to form a stunning mosaic that enraptures the heart of the onlooker and declares to the culture, "Christ saves."

———

Notes.

1. Hideaki Aoyama et al., Macro-Econophysics: New Studies on Economic Networks and Synchronization (Cambridge: Cambridge University Press), 53.

2. Ellen G. White, Sons and Daughters of God (Review and Herald Publishing Association), 286.

Vol. 2

Chapter 13:

PARADOX

"Autonomy and independence involve taking care of yourself—not doing things that diminish you."
- David Schnarch

In the previous chapter, I introduced a simple approach to the doctrine of Christian unity as the one doctrine among all others that—while often ignored in an academic or apologetic sense—happens to be the very one Jesus declared would give traction to his messianic claim. In this sense, the doctrine of Christian unity deserves our focus and attention, perhaps even more than the theological aspects we typically emphasize.

However, before unity can occupy the place Jesus intends it to, we must rid ourselves of faulty perspectives. The fallacy of homogeneity is one of the strongest counterfeits to unity because it creates a cultural expectation where everyone must think, act, and look the same. When this homogeneity is rejected, a person may then be viewed as "less Adventist" or perhaps not Adventist at all. This repressive and coercive vision of unity results not in the attractional and spiritual *enosis* that Jesus calls us to, but in a repulsive cultism that pushes people away from Christ.

However, distancing ourselves from homogeneity is not enough to capture a meaningful vision of Christian unity. Once we recognize that unity thrives in diversity, not in its absence, we must then understand the paradox of attachment and the divine oneness we are called to reflect. These two elements, I have found, are essential in navigating unity within a secular culture.

The Paradox of Attachment

The paradox of attachment is a simple yet profound concept. As human beings, we are relational creatures, designed not only to experience community but also to attach meaning, value, and even a sense of self to that community. In other words, reciprocal relational connection is not something we merely experience externally—it shapes us internally. It transforms who we are, and through emotional bonding with others, we construct a mosaic of our authentic selves.

However, there is an equally true counterpoint: attachment with others only works when a person is differentiated from them.

Recall from our chapters on God that differentiation is an aspect of who he is—God does not derive his value, grandeur, or sense of self from us. He affirms his own existence independent of us while simultaneously loving us more than himself.

Likewise, no human being is truly healthy unless they are differentiated—affirming their own existence irrespective of others. While relational connection brings great value, it does not define the totality of who you are. Your value, identity, and meaning are self-affirmed. You endorse your own existence and do not seek anyone's permission to accept and love yourself as a fully conscious, consequential being. This detachment works in harmony with attachment—while you affirm yourself independently, you also enjoy and desire the company of others. This is the paradox of attachment.

A lack of balanced differentiation often leads to severe relational instability. For example, in *Passionate Marriage*, American psychologist David Schnarch illustrates this with insights from his years as a marriage therapist. He explains that in a marriage, a husband may derive his sense of manhood and worth from his wife's eagerness to respond to him sexually. When she does not, he automatically feels as if his value is being questioned or attacked (this scenario can also be gender-flipped).

Over time, this can lead the husband to pressure his wife for sex, only causing more damage. Schnarch argues that the issue is not mere sexual release but the husband's pursuit of self-affirmation through his wife. This emotional dependence wears the wife down and leads to resentment—while never actually fulfilling the husband's deeper need. True differentiation allows a husband to affirm his own worth without needing his wife to validate it. When she is not in the mood for sex, his sense of value and manhood remains intact because it does not depend on her. In turn, she is liberated from the burden of being responsible for his self-worth. With a differentiated sense of self, the husband can loosen the pressure on his wife, allowing for a healthier, more loving dynamic. The paradox is that, in these scenarios, the husband learns to love himself independently of his wife while simultaneously loving her with all his being.

Returning to the topic of unity, the paradox of attachment means that true unity is manifested in the balance between affirming my own value and existence while maintaining close, intimate proximity to a community I love.

Practically, this means that unity goes far beyond ideological agreement. Even if we share core beliefs, true unity must draw us into a symphonic dance that celebrates the paradox of attachment. I can love you and receive your love while simultaneously existing within an experience of self-affirmed worth. Church, in this sense, is a community in which we are all attached to one another but likewise detached. This allows our relationships to be intimate and deeply defining—without the danger of becoming so emotionally fused that spiritual peer pressure, manipulation, or coercion into a homogenous "standard" takes hold.

All of this can be avoided if, in our pursuit of unity, we learn to derive great meaning from one another while simultaneously refusing to surrender our conscience in the name of "unity" or "acceptance." Instead, we affirm our own experience and existence before God while remaining in close proximity to those who may not always agree with us.

Failure to engage in this paradoxical dance often leads churches to draw rigid lines between who is "in" and who is "out." A conservative church, for example, may only fully accept those who fit its traditionalist mold. Others may attend but never truly feel like they belong. In these scenarios, a guest or young person may feel pressure to abandon their autonomy and instead conform to patterns that, as Schnarch suggests, "diminish you" as a person—all in an effort to be accepted and loved.

The same can happen in contemporary "cool" churches, where only those with the right subcultural expressions feel a sense of belonging. These scenarios are not just about style or fashion—they reflect a deeper issue of uniformity, homogeneity, and the refusal to engage in paradoxical attachment. Humans naturally seek attachment and affirmation from those around them, so they engineer environments where only the people they deem "acceptable" are drawn in while filtering out those they find less valuable.

Borrowing from Schnarch once more, this is what he refers to as *borrowed functioning*—a state in which we "borrow" our sense of self from those around us. This means that the people we surround ourselves with must always be people from whom we can derive value. If I cannot borrow my sense of self from you, then why be around you?

While this may be expected in non-faith environments, the church must transcend this because it is rooted in the ontological character of God's agape love. Our communities should be *trans-carnal*—places where believers derive value from their own relationship with the Creator rather than social validation—while simultaneously loving others wholeheartedly. This kind of environment fosters intergenerational and multicultural fellowship because, in the paradoxical dance, I learn to see those different from me as beautiful beings worth loving more than myself, rather than people from whom I must borrow my value.

However, in the absence of this paradoxical dance, I will always gravitate toward those from whom I can derive meaning, leading to toxic cliques and exclusivist environments. This is why socially awkward individuals, or those who do not fit the dominant subculture, are often ignored. It is why generational tensions emerge—because younger generations do not see older ones as valuable and vice versa. Multiculturalism also suffers, as those with different customs or backgrounds are sidelined. "They're just not my kind of people" becomes code for *I don't get anything out of being around you.*

Embracing the paradox of attachment nurtures an environment that is not only multicultural and intergenerational but also *poly-expressional.* By *poly-expressional,* I mean "many expressions." Every culture contains a variety of subcultures that seldom cross over. In the 90's, this meant the geeks hang out with the geeks, the jocks with the jocks, and the emo's with the emo's. In churches, this often means that the dominant subculture excludes any expression that doesn't align with it.

For example, in a church of upper-class preppy kids, an emo teen may never feel accepted. Likewise, in a church of academic professionals, a blue-collar construction worker may always feel out of place. But if the paradox of attachment is embraced, teens and adults alike will learn to derive meaning from their identity in God rather than from their social circles. This liberates them to invest in relationships with people they would normally overlook.

Because their desire for value is satisfied in Christ, they can now pour love into those whose expressions they would typically find alienating. This fosters *poly-expressional* church environments, where the geek is loved unconditionally even in a youth ministry dominated by sports enthusiasts. Likewise, lawyers and doctors do not attach their meaning and value exclusively to other professionals but welcome the truck driver as one of their own.

In short, the paradox of attachment creates a relational environment in which people are simultaneously attached and detached from one another, fueling an unconditionally accepting culture. Rather than borrowing value from one another, we receive it from Christ. In turn, we begin to see people as inherently worth loving–not because of what they offer our egos but because of who they are.

It is my personal belief that this is the true foundation of an inclusive church–one in which people experience both attachment and detachment in harmony, allowing love to flourish without coercion or exclusion.

The Divine Oneness Reflected

This experience, in turn, gives birth to what I believe true unity is meant to reflect. Jesus said it best in his prayer for the church's unity: *"That all of them may be one, as You,*

Father, are in Me, and I am in You. May they also be in Us, so that the world may believe that You sent Me." (John 17:21)

This text then raises an important question—*to what degree are Jesus and God one?*

For Adventists, the answer is clear: Jesus and God are one, but not in a way that erases their distinct identities. Jesus is not the Father. The Father is not Jesus. And the Holy Spirit is a distinct personality within the Godhead as well. They are one, yet they retain their individuality and authentic selves within that oneness.

I believe this singular-plurality sets the foundation for what true unity looks like in the church. It is not something that can be mandated or coerced. Likewise, a church where everyone looks, thinks, and acts the same—where individual identity is absorbed into a kind of ethereal code—is not true unity at all.

To the contrary, this hyper-attached, homogenous vision of unity aligns more closely with Eastern Hindu metaphysics, where all beings proceed from a universal oneness and ultimately lose their individuality by being reabsorbed into it. This stands in stark contrast to the biblical vision of eternal community in God, where oneness and otherness exist in harmony rather than in opposition.

Ultimately, it is this conceptual dance between oneness and otherness that establishes a vision of unity that is *diverse, differentiated, and biblical* rather than *uniform, coercive, and forced.*

If, as a church, we aim to nurture a culture of oneness and otherness—*unity in diversity, individuality in attachment*—we will manifest a way of being *in and among* that is not only attractive and meaningful but also affirms the messianic claims of Jesus as undoubtedly true.

True Unity in the Fragmented Posthuman Age

As we approach the posthuman era with the many social revolutions that it will bring to the human experience, the topic of unity becomes even more relevant than it has ever been. And make no mistake, it has always been relevant. It has always been the key to the gospel's credibility. But we are entering a world where the very idea of unity is under siege. Not simply because of political divisions or social fractures, but because technology itself is redefining what it means to be *connected* and *human*.

In the posthuman age, unity is not *erased*—it is reengineered. And at the core of that reengineering is a desire among some to achieve a "hivemind society" where neural integration, brain-to-brain interfacing, and AI-assisted group cognition enhance human communication, problem-solving, and even consciousness by merging individual minds into a networked, collective intelligence.[1]

The goal is to create a world with more flourishing for all. But as empire would have it, such ideas are consistently weaponized to serve the interests of those with power and wealth, subordinating the rest of us to a technocratic cult that sees individuality as the antithesis of progress.

Whether a hivemind society ever comes to fruition or not is

a topic of speculation. The truth is, however, we don't have to look that far to see unity being reengineered.

Today, algorithms shape our relationships, ensuring we are only exposed to ideas and people who reinforce our worldview. AI curates our newsfeeds, tailoring reality itself to our biases. Virtual spaces allow us to form relationships without the inconvenience of embodied presence. Gene editing and human enhancement offer the prospect of a *new* unity—not one based on shared humanity, but on engineered perfection and selective enhancement.

The posthuman promise is unity without love, connection without presence, oneness without otherness.

And this is where the church, when properly expressed, becomes radically countercultural.

The early church modeled this beautifully. Slave and free, Jew and Gentile, male and female, rich and poor—all were one in Christ. (Gal. 3:28) This was not an easy, comfortable unity. It was messy, costly, and often painful. And yet, it was real.

And this is the very thing posthumanism cannot offer.

The church then must become a radically embodied community. A community where people are seen, known, and embraced—not as avatars, curated profiles, or filtered selfies, but as *real, flesh-and-blood beings*. A phenomenon that embodies Christ's new humanity. A collective where people experience a new way of being human. A family that offers the weary, vagabond soul a place of belonging.

———

Notes.

1. John Danaher and Steve Petersen, "In Defence of the Hivemind Society," Neuroethics, available at PhilArchive.

Vol. 2

Conclusion

We've covered a lot in this volume. From *The Great Controversy* to the gospel, from the church to remnant theology, from unity to the core question of what it means to be human in an age obsessed with transcendence. But if there's one thread tying it all together, it's this:

Christ is our synthesis.

Everything posthumanism longs for—immortality, transformation, the next evolutionary leap—is already found in him. Not through machine, not through biotech, not through forced progress, but through the fusion of the divine and the human. In him, the mortal is swallowed up by immortality. In him, the future is already breaking into the present.

And yet, instead of living as the community that embodies this future, the church has settled for far less. We've institutionalized what was meant to be a movement. We've commodified what was meant to be a calling. We've reduced salvation to behavior modification when it was meant to be an entirely new way of being.

And that's why we're here. Not to repackage the old in a way that makes it more palatable, but to strip it back to its essence. To rediscover what was always there.

This volume has been about expanding the groundwork for that rediscovery—about reclaiming the story of God in a way that actually answers the questions people are asking. The next volume will take us deeper into what it means to live that story.

What's Next: Volume III

The next seven fundamental beliefs aren't just theological ideas. They are invitations into a way of being that resists the world's counterfeit solutions and offers something infinitely better.

Here's a glimpse of where we're going:

- **Baptism (Belief 15)** – The world is obsessed with reinvention, self-optimization, and becoming the best version of yourself. But what if transformation isn't something you achieve, but something you surrender to?
- **The Lord's Supper (Belief 16)** – We live in a culture where presence is being replaced by digital connection, where food is fuel and nothing more. What does it mean to sit at a table with Jesus, to break real bread, to remember in a way that reshapes reality?
- **Spiritual Gifts and Ministries (Belief 17)** - AI can now write poetry, compose symphonies, and mimic human creativity. If machines can do what we do, what does it mean to be human? And what does it mean to be Spirit-empowered in a world of AI powered humans (via Neuralink etc.)?
- **The Gift of Prophecy (Belief 18)** – We live in the midst of a Christian Nationalist resurgence. What

does it mean to speak prophetically in this context. What does it mean to resist the allure of power and protest the corruption of church and state?

- **The Law of God (Belief 19)** – The modern world sees moral law as oppressive, an outdated system designed to control. But what if the law was never about control? What if it was about freedom?
- **The Sabbath (Belief 20)** – We are addicted to speed, to productivity, to hustle culture. Even rest has been commodified—marketed as self-care and monetized through wellness apps. What does it mean to actually *stop*? What does it mean to live in sacred time?
- **Stewardship (Belief 21)** – The economy is built on scarcity. The world is built on taking. What does it mean to live as people who don't hoard, who don't exploit, who don't consume without thought? What does it mean to be people of abundance in a culture of fear?

The Future is Now

So much of the modern world is built on fear—fear of death, fear of irrelevance, fear of missing out, fear of not being enough. That's why posthumanism exists. It's an attempt to solve a problem that has already been solved.

Jesus is the firstborn of a new humanity. The remnant isn't an institution. It's not a club. It's not a brand. It's a people who live as if *the future has already arrived*. A people who embody something so radically different that the world takes notice.

We don't need to compete with Silicon Valley's vision of the future. We need to show the world that the future has already broken in, in Jesus.

And we get to live it now.

Pastor Marcos | The Story Church Project

"hidden."

At Pentecost, the early church was a disruptive force, challenging the status quo. But today, it's become a program within four walls, disconnected from its missional calling, feeling irrelevant, and losing its youth.

But the story isn't over.

God is stirring, His Spirit is at work, and a new generation is rising to reclaim the church's radical essence. In "hidden.", Pastor Marcos, a missional church planter, calls the church back to its true identity, revealing that the best is yet to come - and you and I are a part of it.

Go to:
https://www.thestorychurchproject.com/books

www.ingramcontent.com/pod-product-compliance
Lightning Source LLC
Chambersburg PA
CBHW062105080426
42734CB00012B/2763